The Spirituality
of Transformation,
Joy, and Justice

THE SPIRITUALITY OF TRANSFORMATION, JOY, AND JUSTICE

THE IGNATIAN WAY FOR EVERYONE

Patrick Saint-Jean, SJ

Broadleaf Books

Minneapolis

THE SPIRITUALITY OF TRANSFORMATION, JOY, AND JUSTICE
The Ignatian Way for Everyone

Library of Congress Control Number 2023008899 (print)

Cover design: 1517 Media

Print ISBN: 978-1-5064-9115-8
eBook ISBN: 978-1-5064-9116-5

Printed in China

Contents

Stage II: Jesus as a Role Model

Stage III: Suffering and Death

Foreword

Have you ever seen friends in an entirely unexpected setting—and for a split second failed to recognize them? For me, reading this book was something like that. I've been a Jesuit for more than thirty years, and during that time, the life and teachings of Saint Ignatius of Loyola, the founder of the Jesuits, has been my foundation—and yet this book managed to surprise me with new insights.

Patrick Saint-Jean, SJ, is my friend and brother in the Society of Jesus; he is also a fellow-worker in the struggle for justice. Over the years I have known him, I've been impressed by the ways in which he integrates his deep immersion in Ignatian spirituality, his commitment to academic rigor in the field of psychology, and his cultural background; this integration had led to a powerful new voice that speaks to our world's most urgent issues. Patrick is uniquely positioned to describe Ignatian spirituality from the perspectives of both a practitioner and a psychoanalyst—and he does so with humor, sensitivity, and vulnerability. In this, he follows in the footsteps of Saint Ignatius, who taught that we can find God even in surprising and unsuspected places.

Like all Christians, we Jesuits are encouraged to be "all things to all people" (1 Corinthians 9:23), and that is what Patrick does in this book. He leaves behind the academic and religious vocabulary that comes so naturally to him, and instead, like a good translator who knows the idioms and lexicon of a different language, he frames the basics of Ignatian spirituality with words that are accessible to any reader, regardless of their religious background (or lack thereof). Today, when many people are disillusioned with organized religion, this book offers a nourishing meal of meaning and truth that will be as palatable to the "spiritual-but-not-religious" reader as it is to the more traditional seeker of spiritual substance.

Also, the "Pause" sections at the end of each chapter offer inspiration, encouragement and direction that are exceedingly practical, no matter where you are in your spiritual journey. You may be a newcomer to the path or a seasoned traveler; either way, you will find Patrick's new book to be as useful as if you had a wise and perceptive companion walking with you on your journey.

In this book, you'll find a framework for both self-understanding and for community-building. You'll see how interaction with the Divine (however you understand that concept) is interwoven with the daily challenge to build a kinder, more just world. The book's accessibility and its adaptability, combined with the beauty and resonance of its simple language, are gifts to all readers—including you!

—JAMES MARTIN, SJ
New York City, 2023

Introduction

The Journey to Your True Self

Psychologists agree: we all need to be more conscious of what's going on "inside" us, in that invisible part of ourselves we call the mind. We may fear what we will find when we look inside ourselves, but, as psychologist Ann Weiser Cornell said, "There are no enemies inside. Every part of us is trying to save our lives." We can trust our inner selves to know what's best for us—but first, we have to get to know them.

Back in the 1960s, Dr. Cornell was one of a group of researchers at the University of Chicago who found that people with greater inner awareness had better mental health. More recent studies have determined that the habit of self-reflection contributes to increased levels of compassion, creativity, work productivity, and self-confidence. People who take time for inner consciousness have better decision-making skills, communicate better with others, and form stronger and happier relationships. The answers we seek in our external lives can often be found inside ourselves—and, according to Carl Jung, the founder of analytical psychology, when we look inside, we can even find God there.

Long before the development of modern psychology, Ignatius of Loyola, the sixteenth-century Spanish mystic who founded the Society of Jesus (the Jesuits), also believed that inner awareness was essential to a meaningful and healthy life. In fact, Ignatius developed an entire structure around the practice of turning inward—what he called "interior recollection."

Today, we usually connect "recollection" with "memory"—but in the sixteenth century, the word referred more broadly to gathering together something that had been scattered. Interior recollection, in other words, is a way to bring focus to our inner worlds, including our memories, our random thoughts, our emotions, our inclinations and desires, and our imaginings. Recollection orders our mental chaos, creating clarity and a sense of our priorities, which then give meaning and direction to our external actions. Interior recollection—turning inward in a habitual and structured way—becomes a container that generates the transformation of both our inner and outer lives.

Ignatius believed that in the same way that we strengthen our bodies' health and development with certain behaviors, so too the inner person—what he called the *soul*—can be encouraged to grow through specific practices. Ignatius was so convinced that careful, even methodical inner awareness is essential to the well-lived life that he wrote a structured set of meditations, prayers, and mental practices. He based these practices—or exercises—on his own experience, using a form of what would one day be called the scientific method to test and record the behaviors and thoughts he'd found most effective for deepening and empowering the inner life. The center point of what Ignatius called the Spiritual Exercises was the life of Jesus, as it is described in the Bible's four Gospels.

Although Ignatius wrote *The Spiritual Exercises* some five hundred years ago, they remain relevant and useful today. As twenty-first-century seekers of meaning, we do not need to be Jesuit, Catholic, or even Christian to make use of Ignatius's methods; the Spiritual Exercises inspired some of history's most important thinkers, from René Descartes to Carl Jung. The Exercises's principles are found within Alcoholics Anonymous Twelve-Step Program, as well as in many mindfulness practices. According to Jesuit scholar William M. Watson, Ignatius's insights are similar to recently developed psychological methods that have "proven effective to reprogram and balance the biochemical systems of the brain, even after years of depression and addiction."

The inner growth that results from engaging with the Exercises is spiritual and psychological, but at the same time, this deep development of our interior selves shapes our exterior actions and behaviors, leading to transformation in our everyday relationships and responsibilities. The Exercises nurture well-balanced and healthy lives infused with meaning and purpose. They meet us where we are, no matter where we are in our spiritual journeys. We do not need to conform to any doctrine, theology, or standard of sanctity in order to begin.

The Foundation

Ignatius began his structured set of meditations, prayers, and mental practices by explaining his primary assumptions.

These are the most basic ideas we need to understand before beginning the Spiritual Exercises.

The Divine Spirit is everywhere, present in all things.

Ignatius firmly believed there is no division between "spiritual" and "physical" realities, nor are there separate supernatural and natural worlds or sacred and secular realms because *all* things are different expressions of the same Spirit. The Divine Spirit manifests both tangibly and intangibly; it is present in every aspect of life, every interaction, and every object. Love is the current that animates human beings and earthworms, stars and microbes, trees and planets. The entire world is alive with meaning.

Reverence and stewardship are the natural outgrowths of a Spirit-infused reality.

Because God is in everything, our spiritual identities are lived out in ordinary life—in household chores, job responsibilities, creative expression, and human relationships. Each aspect of our lives then becomes a source of connection to a deeper reality, an opening into wonder and mystery. At the same time, as we realize all things are sacred, we feel a greater sense of responsibility and respect for the world around us. Acts of social and environmental justice are the natural results of this vision.

Balance is essential to a healthy life that weaves together both the inner and outer aspects of our experience.

Ignatius lived in an age when fasting and other forms of severe physical discipline were considered useful spiritual practices, much more so than they are today. He was the sort of guy who threw himself wholeheartedly into things, often going to excess, but he learned from experience that too much "spiritual discipline" can be bad for the body. Having benefited from his own failures, he taught that when we neglect the needs of our physical bodies, our spiritual lives also suffer—and then we are not able to joyfully and effectively carry out the active stewardship and participation in life to which we are called. On the other hand, we also need to practice balance when it comes to our various external responsibilities, not allowing ourselves to be consumed or driven by the many demands we face. This teaching of Ignatius is similar to the Buddhist "Middle Way," a road that neither removes us from the outer world nor allows us to get lost in it. Both perspectives point toward living in such a way that we are fully engaged with the particularities of each moment, while at the same time, we remain grounded in our inner connection to a larger realm of reality.

The life of Jesus, rather than any aspect of our inner or outer lives, creates a focal point for a balanced life.

When Ignatius tells us to use Jesus's life as a focal point for spiritual growth, our first reaction may be reluctance. We may assume Ignatius wants us to distance ourselves from our own lives' tangible pleasures in order to focus on something—or someone—abstract from the ancient past. This was not the meaning Ignatius intended. He wanted his followers to be fully engaged in life, but he also knew that human beings tend to rely on many things to make sense of their lives—jobs, relationships, reputations, possessions, to name just a few—when ultimately, none of these things endure or satisfy.

Because our lives are constantly changing, we will inevitably be frustrated, disappointed, depressed, or even traumatized if we depend on any single person, thing, or activity as the focal point of our helter-skelter lives. Having a focus that lies outside our own interests allows us to step back from the changing circumstances around us. Again, this foundation of Ignatian spirituality is very similar to a Buddhist understanding, this time the practice of detachment. When we don't cling to a particular outcome or circumstance, we are free to truly enjoy and participate in whatever *is*.

Jesus's life of love and self-surrender offers us the consummate example of this way of life. Modeling our lives on his provides an anchor that remains steady, even in the midst of life's continual changes.

Inner awareness creates freedom

Although we sometimes think of religious practices as restricting our freedom, Ignatius believed the Divine Spirit is actually the source of all liberty, allowing us to be the truest and best versions of ourselves. This is a freedom that encompasses every circumstance of our life, and it is already inherently ours—yet we must search for it through inner work. We can only find it if we release our insistence on the selfish desires that can enslave and entrap us.

The Spiritual Exercises are intended to free us from the tyranny of our own likes, dislikes, comforts, desires, drives, appetites, and passions so that we can become the unique expression of the Spirit who lives in each of us. From one perspective, this requires a deep transformation of who we are, but at the same time, it is also the recovery of who we *always were*. We each reclaim the "self" we were created to be, the essential nature that existed before life's pressures clouded our awareness.

The Stages

Ignatius divided the Exercises into a thirty-day journey containing four thematic "weeks":

Week 1 focuses on the brokenness in the world and within ourselves.

Week 2 looks at why and how Jesus becomes a center point of personhood and wisdom, a reliable guide and role model.

Week 3 confronts the reality of human suffering and death.

Week 4 affirms the joyful hope of new life.

After the final week, Ignatius included one more exercise, which focuses on the meaning of Divine love.

While Ignatius intended his exercises to be practiced week by week, over the course of a month, twenty-first-century life is not conducive to committing thirty consecutive days to an intense period of spiritual reflection. Ignatius himself made allowance for adapting the exercises in various ways to meet individual needs, and this book is intended, likewise, as an offering of an adaptive journey. Read it at whatever speed works best for you, but please do not rush! Take a month, two months, or a year—but commit to spending time regularly with Ignatius's spiritual road map.

I will refer to each of Ignatius's four "weeks" as a "stage" in the inner journey, with Ignatius's final exercise serving as the fifth and final stage. Instead of breaking these down into thirty "days," we will use chapters, with each distinct stage having five chapters. Keep in mind—this isn't intended to be the sort of book you read from cover to cover in one or two sittings. Instead, you might want to set aside an hour in your schedule, either every day, once a week, or a few times a week, to sit down with a single chapter, taking time to engage with it fully. In this way, one chapter at a time, you can work your way consecutively through the book's five stages.

The Examen

One of the spiritual tools Ignatius included in the Spiritual Exercises is the "Examen," an opportunity to engage more deeply with our own lives. This practice is usually outlined in five steps:

1. **Become grounded in the present moment.** Experience the sacredness of *now*. Consciously open yourself to the spiritual light that sees through all subterfuges and evasions.
2. **Look back at your day with a sense of gratitude.** Even if your day held painful or challenging moments, gratitude is the key that can open up the positive potential of each circumstance.
3. **Take some time to become aware of your own emotions.** Identify your feelings with honesty and unconditional acceptance rather than judgment or guilt.
4. **Look to see if you have done harm to anyone with your words or actions.** Now acknowledge any moments during the day when you allowed the selfish or self-serving aspects of yourself to gain control of your life.
5. **Resolve to do better in the future.** Think of specific, practical action you can take tomorrow, not only to make amends for today's mistakes but also to more fully manifest the full potential of your life.

Ignatius was so impressed by the effectiveness of the Examen that he required his followers to engage in it twice a day: during their midday break and at night before going to sleep. He intended this to become habitual practice, a few moments of interior reflection embedded in every day. He himself, according to one of his companions, went so far as to practice the Examen hourly.

Although the Examen was originally labeled as "an examination of conscience," implying that its chief purpose was to direct our attention to our failures and misdeeds, a more modern understanding of Ignatius's intention is that of an "examination of *consciousness*." In other words, it's a tool to help us bring more of our lives into conscious awareness; it's a useful lens for bringing focus and order to our jumbled thoughts. Each chapter of this book ends with a "pause"—a few moments to stop reading and instead reflect on one or two Examen-based questions.

Falling in Love

According to a quotation usually attributed to Pedro Arrupe, a former superior general of the Jesuits, the end goal of Ignatius's teaching is "falling in love in a quite absolute way."

> What you are in love with, what seizes your imagination, will affect everything. It decides what will get you

out of bed in the morning, what you will do with your evenings, how you will spend your weekends, what you read, who you know, what breaks your heart, and what amazes you with joy and gratitude. Fall in love, stay in love and it will decide everything.

And so, I invite you to fall in love with your life in a new way. As you journey with the Spiritual Exercises, may you discover a sense of joyful meaning that gives clarity and direction. May love renew you and transform you. May it change you so that you can change our world.

Stage I:

Our Broken World

1

Missing the Mark

*As I begin the work of inner and outer transformation,
I will first seek to become conscious of anything
that diminishes or damages my identity or my relationships.*

If you're like me, you probably don't find sin an appealing topic. It's a place where most of us would rather not begin. Even talking about sin can bring a cloud of guilt we'd rather not face; the word implies we're bad people, possibly bound straight for hell. And yet this is where Ignatius begins his first stage of the Spiritual Exercises, offering a meditation that invites us to look with clarity at the ways in which cosmic (universal) sin and personal sin shape both the state of our world and the state of ourselves. This, said Ignatius, is actually the most important place to begin.

In the Bible, the Hebrew and Greek words translated as "sin" meant, literally, "missing the mark." This conveys an image of an archer sighting her arrow at a target, pulling back her bow, releasing the arrow . . . and missing the bull's eye. There's no shame in this image, only the reality that human behaviors, both individually and as societies, repeatedly fall short of our ideal goals. Missing the mark exposes us and those around us to harm, to diminishment. It makes us stray from the path that leads to healing and well-being.

We work to be "good" people, kind to others and generous with our resources—but we get caught up in our selfish urges; all too often, we'd rather stroke our own egos than concern ourselves with other people. At the societal level, we claim to value justice and freedom, and yet too many of us experience the daily effects of injustice and oppression. These profound disparities are the consequences of walking outside the healing path; they are failures to hit our target.

Another way to think of sin is as something that damages our wholeness and well-being, either as individuals or as communities. Here again, we have an ideal reality (a healing path, a target we aim for), a shining beautiful world of thriving relationships (between humans; between humans and nonhumans, including the entire planet on which we live; and between humans and the Source of all life). Sin consists of anything that damages those thriving relationships, that beautiful world.

Missing the mark leads to division rather than solidarity. It makes us believe our differences are more important than all the things we have in common. Focused on ourselves and our desires, we become careless with our words and actions, and selfish with our resources. As we damage the living bonds of relationship, we ultimately create a broken world, a world of poverty, racism, sexism, violence, and anger. Our reluctance to recognize and protect our connections has also polluted our air, water, and soil, putting our entire planet at risk.

It's easy to dismiss our small, daily acts of selfishness as unimportant. I, for one, am unlikely to murder another human being. I also like to think I wouldn't stand by and watch while someone was assaulted, that instead, I would jump in to protect and defend. And yet the society in which we live literally kills people by favoring white systems of power and denying Black, brown, and Indigenous communities adequate medical care and legal protection. Environmental destruction combines with these factors to create mortality rates higher than white people's.

Societal problems like these can seem so overwhelming and complicated that we throw up our hands in helpless despair. And by doing nothing, we support this ongoing loss of life. Too often, the choices we make—in terms of our lifestyles, the things we purchase, the way we use our time, and our community involvement, to name just a few—all say we don't really care. If we truly cared, we'd do something.

On a personal level, we might also think of sin as anything that clouds or warps the Divine image we each are meant to carry within us. In this sense, sin robs us of our true identities, to the point we sometimes forget who we really are. Unhealthy behaviors seem to offer solutions to the emptiness we feel inside, but they are only mirages. No matter how much we work, play, eat, drink, buy, or wear, we still sense that something is missing inside us.

In this very first step of the Spiritual Exercises, Ignatius invites us to reflect on all the ways we have missed the mark. He asks us to look first at our personal stories, and then at how we have been complicit within the larger arena of our society's history. He also challenges us to see how these stories are interconnected.

In doing this, Ignatius isn't offering us something negative and distasteful. Instead, he calls us to wake up to our true identities, our authentic Divine natures. When we do so, we look to see what is holding us back from being whole and healthy. We learn to ask important questions:

- *Where have we missed the target of loving relationships and respectful connections?*
- *Where does our society fall short of that goal?*
- *How does our society influence our behaviors and attitudes, even as our own inner selfishness contributes to our society's failures?*

These problems don't have easy answers. Ignatius never claimed an easy-answer approach. But he did understand we cannot focus on becoming whole without first taking a clear-eyed, objective look at our reality. We cannot work to build a better world, a world of interconnection and mutual respect, without looking to see the specific places where our society is broken.

We do this not by obsessing over the negative with a sense of guilt and shame but by fixing our eyes on the positive with energy and enthusiasm. Remember, an archer becomes more skillful by focusing on the target. In doing so, she needs to be aware of everything that might interfere with her aim—but her gaze stays on the bull's eye. Despite distractions around her and within her, she sharpens that focus until she is certain her arrow will fly true and straight.

"Become aware," Ignatius says to us. "This awareness is the beginning of your transformation. It is the first step toward justice and joy—and it is also an ongoing path you must follow until it becomes a way of life."

Pause

As we begin a spiritual self-improvement "program," we may be tempted to focus on an idealistic image of ourselves, the people we think we *should* be. Ignatius says instead, *Start wherever you are.*

Take a moment to quiet yourself. Focusing on your breath helps to do this. When you feel settled, look at your life and see if you can list two or three things that are pushing you out of alignment with the healthy, joyful person you were intended to be. Don't be vague or generic; focus on specifics—but don't allow yourself to go beyond two or three things. Once you have identified them, hold each of these things, one by one, in your consciousness.

Now examine each one more closely. Look at them honestly but gently, with an attitude of curiosity rather than denial or guilt. What do they tell you about yourself? How do they interfere with your relationships with others (including your relationships with the nonhuman world and with your sense of the Divine)? How are they connected to the society in which you live?

As you do this, do not shift your attention to how to "fix" these aspects of yourself. Instead, simply allow your consciousness of each thing to deepen and deepen. This can be scary, but try to disconnect yourself from your emotional reactions. This doesn't mean you should force your emotions to be something they aren't. Instead, step back and regard your feelings with the same curiosity you've been using all along in this exercise.

Finally, even after you have set this book aside, continue to examine these two or three things that are making you "miss the mark." Make small pauses in the days ahead to come back to them again and again. (Maybe while you're driving, standing in line at a store, or waiting on hold on the phone.) Discover everything you can from each distraction or obstacle. Make a note of anything you have learned, perhaps in a journal, so you won't forget.

2

Unconditionally Loved

As I open myself to the understanding
that I am unconditionally loved,
I will also open my mind
to the new possibilities love brings.

As a young man in the military, Ignatius was something of a party animal. After a serious battle injury, he was confined to a long period of recovery in bed, and during that time, he encountered the love of God. This first encounter began his journey of transformation, but in the months and years that followed, he still had much to learn about the nature of love.

Like all of us, Ignatius had made up stories in his head about who God is. These stories are usually based on our own experiences, and in Ignatius's case, chivalry was the only model he had for Divine love. His mother had died when he was very young, his father was domineering but distant, and so at first, Ignatius based the only story he knew how to tell about the Divinity on the one-way loyalty and sacrifice of the knight for his king.

This limited understanding of love was enough to set Ignatius on a new path for his life, but it was not enough to sustain his ongoing spiritual journey. His misunderstanding of Divine love made him profoundly judgmental of others—and he turned that same harsh judgment on himself, sinking deeper and deeper into depression and guilt.

And then light broke through his confusion. He realized Divine love is abundant and unquestioning. God never looks at us with disapproval and disgust, for real love gives itself away lavishly without questions or conditions.

By the time Ignatius finished writing *The Spiritual Exercises*, he knew the realization of love belongs here, at the very beginning of our spiritual journeys. The awareness of unlimited love allows us to look within ourselves without fear. It changes the way we see ourselves, but it also changes the way we see everything else. Wrapped in the security of Divine love, we are able, as Ignatius put it, to "embrace salvation."

From a biblical perspective, in Hebrew and Christian scriptures, *salvation* is a Divine initiative operating within human history. It's a little like a chemical reaction that's slowly but surely transforming our world into the realm of God. Some religious language limits what is meant by *salvation* to a future when we see God in the eternal rejoicing of the afterlife, but Ignatius, like Jesus and also Moses, understood "salvation" to be something that starts to happen here, in this life, an ongoing, unfolding process of healthy growth. The Greek word translated as "salvation" in the Gospels generally refers to deliverance from all that holds us back from healing and wholeness. Salvation comes from the gift of Divine love as it interweaves with the call to love, putting us on the path by which we grow into the people we were always intended to be, the healthiest and truest versions of ourselves.

We are each broken in some way—but at the same time, we are unconditionally loved, accepted, and affirmed by the Source of all life. Love is the energy of the universe. When we open ourselves to love, it flows into each one of us, and then out into the world around us.

This love that Ignatius saw as the gateway into the spiritual life is not an emotion so much as a commitment, one that always leads to active relationship. We cannot find inner healing and happiness if our interactions with others are unhealthy or judgmental—and vice versa: our relationships will not be healthy and growing if we do not accept and care for ourselves. "Love your neighbor as you love yourself": these might be the most well-known words that Jesus spoke. Jesus, and then Ignatius after him, held that we cannot truly love anyone, including the Divine, if we do not love ourselves—and we cannot truly love ourselves if we refuse to love other people. Love by its very nature cannot be hoarded; it has to be shared.

The world Ignatius envisioned is a network of loving relationship. Love is the Source, sweeping us all up into a story far greater than anything we had ever imagined. This living, breathing network has no room in it for intolerance or oppression, for it includes everyone. Everyone is needed. No one is left out. Cooperation and mutual support are its lifeblood.

Love does not erase or minimize our need to face all the ways we "miss the mark." Instead, it frees us from the need to prove our value through competition; our self-image no longer depends on success (usually defined by comparing ourselves to others), and so our emotional and physical energy is freed to find new purpose. Love gives direction to our lives, leading us away from the narrow world of oppression and injustice, as it takes us into new realms of equality, kindness, and unlimited possibility.

Pause

Take a moment to quiet yourself. Breathe in, breathe out. When you feel your mind is quiet, ask yourself: *What story have I been telling myself about love?*

We all have these stories. We use them to make sense of our lives. But often these narratives need to be enlarged to make room for new ideas and possibilities. So ask yourself now: *How has the story I've been telling restricted or limited my life? What assumptions has it made that have detracted from rather than enhanced my self-worth?*

Our childhood caregivers are usually the initial source of the stories we tell about our lives, about love, and about the Divine. Take a moment to think about your relationship with the adults in your life when you were growing up. Then take a little time to consider: *How do these relationships continue to shape the narrative of my life? Are there any assumptions I've been making—about life, about myself and others, about God—that I now need to discard or expand?*

The experience of unconditional love is ongoing, continuing to unfold throughout our lives. Ask yourself now: *If my life were based on an ever-deepening awareness of unconditional love, how would that change things? What might I attempt? How would I look at others differently?*

Finally, as love rules out the possibility of injustice and oppression, it comes into conflict with the reality of our world as it is today. Take a few moments to wonder: *Where in my community do I see an opportunity for love to bring change and healing? How might I participate in that?* Bring those questions with you as you return to the world outside this book; continue to reflect on them, and be alert to any glimmers of answers that bring light to your path forward.

3

Self-Awareness

*While I seek to grow in my understanding and expression
of love, I will also work to be increasingly aware
of anything within me that holds me back,
as well as anything that propels me forward.*

When Ignatius first decided to change the direction of
his life, he stumbled over the guilt he felt about things
he had done in the past. He wasn't being hard on himself out
of false humility—the old Ignatius had done some pretty bad
stuff—but now, his ever-busy, creative mind came up with
strategies for dealing with his guilt. With his usual fervor, he

launched himself into a strict program of self-denial. Unfortunately, his strategies were self-destructive rather than life-giving and healthy.

Then, like so many spiritual leaders, he had an experience that felt like waking up—like leaving a nightmare existence and opening his eyes to a world of light. He realized that the way to enter into relationship with the Source of life was not by looking backward at his old behaviors but by paying attention to the *now* of his inner and outer realities.

"The road to hell is paved with good intentions" is an old and familiar saying—but it might be more accurate to say, "The road to hell (to unhappiness, emptiness, and despair) is paved with a *lack of intention*." When our lives have no focus, they often seem random and rushed. As we fail to pay attention to the reality of our inner and outer lives, we lose our sense of control. We allow circumstances to push us back and forth. We lack the strength of our own inner authority.

One aspect of self-awareness requires identifying the faulty narratives we discussed in the last chapter, the falsehoods we've been telling ourselves about who we are, about the nature of love, and about what the Divine is like. To recognize what's really going on, we take an objective look at ourselves, as though we were spectators to our own stories.

In quiet moments of reflection, we stand back and observe our own thoughts and actions.

Many self-help practices and religious traditions emphasize that this ongoing self-audit is essential rather than optional. In the Twelve-Step program, the fourth step is to make a "searching and fearless inventory of myself," and then that process continues in step ten. The Qur'an teaches that if we want to know the Giver of Life, we must first know ourselves. Hinduism speaks of the call to know the inmost Self, the Divine Reality that exists within each person. The Christian scriptures tell us to "examine ourselves" and "take every thought captive," so that our mental processes align with Divine love. Pagan teachers describe "embodied cognition," in which we become aware of the ways in which our physical selves, our thoughts, and the world around us interact and shape each other. Most Indigenous religions, from Africa to the Americas, focus on understanding the self within a living web of relationships; according to this perspective, we can only know our inner selves within the context of our connections to one another, to the Earth, and to the Divine Spirit. Judaism has a similar belief, called *Tikkun Middot*, which is the process of first seeing ourselves clearly and then bringing our interior selves into exterior reality through loving, trustworthy connections. From a Buddhist perspective, self-awareness is the practice of intentional "mindfulness"—by which the Buddha meant a continuous awareness of whatever you are giving your attention to, which he viewed not as an end in itself but as the essential foundation for living an ethical life. Psychological research points to similar conclusions; Allan Fenigstein, who has studied self-awareness for more than forty years, says it is both a "tool and goal" that leads to both greater emotional health and an enhanced ability to get along in the workplace, the home, and the larger community.

Science has found that attention even shapes our brain patterns. By changing where we give our attention, we can also change the interaction of our neurons, laying down new pathways—which translates into new thought habits as well as new behaviors. This requires constant practice. Since our inner and outer lives are always changing, self-awareness isn't something we can do once and be done with. It's an ongoing activity that's based on patience and commitment.

The Gospel of Thomas (a collection of pithy sayings attributed to Jesus that was not accepted by the church as a "canonical" Gospel) has a line of wisdom that speaks to this sense of loving and honoring the self: "If you bring forth what is within you, what you bring forth will save you.

If you do not bring forth what is within you, what you do not bring forth will destroy you." As we bring into consciousness the false narratives and hidden assumptions that otherwise define our lives, we find new well-being at many levels of our lives (emotionally, spiritually, relationally).

Inner self-awareness also leads to more sharply defined goals. Ignatius knew that when we understand the true desires of our hearts, we can pursue them with greater focus and energy. Understanding ourselves allows us to see our own longings more clearly.

Awareness also helps us recognize anything within us that holds us back. It might be a lack of self-confidence, an addiction to a certain unhealthy or counterproductive behavior, a need to be better than others, or a selfish urge to acquire more money, more things, more prestige. Whatever it is, self-knowledge allows us to step back from these unhelpful behaviors and attitudes and see them for what they really are—barriers to the experience and expression of love.

As we look inside ourselves, we come to realize the heart's true desire that lies behind each inner obstacle to a life of love. Our lack of self-confidence may spring from the childhood narratives we created about ourselves. Our addictions are the gnarled and twisted expressions of our longing for meaning and intimacy. Both the need to be better than others and the desire for wealth may go back to the same lack of self-esteem, expressing our deep need for unconditional love. By identifying our true desires, the healthy roots behind their poisoned expressions, and focusing on them, we identify what moves us to wholehearted engagement. In doing so, we gain motivation and stamina for action and change.

Ignatius's call for inner awareness didn't focus only on the problem areas we discover within ourselves. Self-awareness also allows us to identify our genuine strengths and talents. As we free these from the ego's frantic voice (*Am I any good at that? Am I better at it than he is? Should I let people know I can do that—or will I sound conceited?*), we allow our abilities to have greater expression. We use our skills with authority in service to the demands of love.

Again, this is a process: always progressive, never absolute. This is why Ignatius stressed making the Examen (described in the introduction) a daily practice. Awareness can only be found in the *now*, which is constantly changing. Each time you practice the Examen, it will have something new to show you. The same is true of the Spiritual Exercises. If you return to this book in a few years, you will be at a new point in your spiritual journey, which means you will bring something different to the Exercises (and you will take away something new from them as well).

The goal of the spiritual life, Ignatius believed, was to "choose what better leads to God's deepening life" within us. Self-awareness furthers that goal. It allows us to make room for the unconditional love of our Source. It empowers us to choose what we really want for our lives.

Pause

Begin by finding a place and time where you won't be disturbed. Sit in a comfortable chair or on the floor with your legs crossed. Set a timer on your phone or computer for ten minutes.

Now direct your awareness to your breath; feel the air moving in and out of your body as you breathe, and notice your belly rising and falling as the air enters and leaves your body.

When you feel quiet and settled, draw your attention inward, to your thoughts. Notice every thought that comes and goes—but do not get lost in pursuing each thought. Simply observe it, recognize it, and let it go. Make a mental note of each thought, but when you feel tempted to keep thinking about something, bring your attention back to your breath until you feel focused again. Be gentle but firm with yourself.

When the timer signals that ten minutes have gone by, take a moment to reflect on anything you realized about yourself and your thoughts.

As you repeat this exercise on a daily basis, you may want to extend the length of time—but do not push yourself to do something that isn't comfortable for you. Practicing self-awareness should be a life-giving activity that brings you greater understanding of yourself and others. It's not meant to be something you do as a form of rigid self-discipline or spiritual heroism; when we push ourselves too hard or fast on our inner journeys, spiritual practices often become so unappealing that we retreat, letting our attention return to its normal scattered and unaware state.

4

Emotions

I will not hide, run away from, or deny my emotions.
Instead, wrapped in the security of Divine love,
I will learn healthier and more constructive ways
to interact with my feelings.

In the early days of Ignatius's spiritual adventure, he often encountered emotional hurdles that slowed him down. Alongside the headlong passion that drove him so relentlessly, he was also a pragmatic realist, and so he pondered how to proceed on his inner journey with greater efficiency. Eventually, he realized the very things that made his spiritual life difficult—his emotions, which he called the "movements of the soul"—were also essential to his relationship with the Source of his life. He came to believe these soul movements are one way the Divine Spirit communicates with us.

At the same time, Ignatius recognized that not all emotions facilitated his spiritual life. Instead, they interfered with his consciousness of unconditional love; they clouded his perception of the ways he had "missed the mark" in his interactions with others, and they interrupted the inner scrutiny that led him to the Divine Spirit within him. Ignatius called these unhelpful emotions "disordered." He did not call them "bad" or "sinful"—but he saw that our emotions can become so disorganized and overwhelming that they run our lives.

We don't have to let disordered emotions push us around. Instead, as we become aware of these unruly feelings, Ignatius believed, we can put them back in order. This does not mean repressing them or denying them but just the opposite: we pay close attention to our emotions in order to hear what they are saying to us.

We need to hear the real message, though, and not just the story we have made up about it. We often think our inner feelings are reporting on the outer world. If we're depressed, we tell ourselves a story about the hopelessness of the world—but when our emotions shift and we feel happy, then the world around us seems brighter and more hopeful too. In reality, the world stays pretty much the same; only our inner feelings change. The same sort of thing happens with other emotions: if we find ourselves getting in a rage whenever we think about politics, feeling on edge when we're around certain people, or being frightened when we read the news, our emotions are our reactions to these things rather than the things themselves. We'd like to put the blame on circumstances or other people, but Ignatius challenges us to take responsibility for our soul movements, recognizing their true sources.

From an evolutionary perspective, emotions are a little like our five senses. Just as eyesight, touch, hearing, taste, and smell make us aware of the world around us, emotions also allow us to detect stimuli in our environment and then adjust our actions accordingly. When a ferocious animal was chasing our long-long-ago ancestor, fear let her know she should run away and find safety. When she felt happy after being close to other human beings, she worked to strengthen these connections, and in doing so, she increased her chances of survival.

Today, emotions still function in a similar way. Our inner feelings get our attention. They point out things we should be noticing, things we might otherwise overlook. When our emotions are overwhelming and disorderly, though, they cloud our perception instead of enhancing it. And they produce stress, that plague of modern life.

Stress is a warped version of our healthy reflex to physical danger, what we call our fight-or-flight response. It's our reaction to life when it seems like too much for us to handle—when we're too busy, too lonely, too tired, too distracted, too frustrated, too whatever. Notice that once again, we're making a narrative that puts the blame on our exterior lives—our jobs are too demanding, people don't like us, there are too many interruptions in our day, things just don't ever seem to go right—when really, it's not our outer realities that are causing stress. It's our *reactions* to those realities.

Our evolutionary response to danger includes elevated blood pressure, rapid breath and heartbeat, tense muscles, and hyper-alertness—but these reactions were intended to last only a short time, getting our bodies ready to either fight or run away. Instead, in the modern world, we often live our lives in a constant state of low-grade anxiety where neither running away nor fighting is an option. Meanwhile, the effects of stress eat away at our health. Our bodies weren't built for running on overdrive.

Stress is the expression of disordered emotion. Intentional consciousness of our inner lives, including our emotions, is the antidote. Awareness is the first step in bringing order to chaos.

Psychologists consider emotional intelligence to be the ability to understand, use, and recognize emotions in positive ways that relieve stress, while helping us communicate more effectively, demonstrate compassion, overcome challenges, and find creative solutions to conflict. Long before anyone defined emotional intelligence, however, Ignatius already understood both the pitfalls and the potential of our emotional lives.

He saw that despite our tendency to label some emotions as positive and others as negative, *all* emotions can become dysregulated and destructive, and *all* emotions can also be used in positive ways to enhance our lives. Sometimes the so-called positive emotions can mislead us (when, for example, we feel glad about another person's misfortune, or when we are so contented that we ignore our world's desperate need for justice and care)—and sometimes negative emotions can show us the way. Anger can wake us up to the oppression and inequality around us. Sorrow can bring us awareness of our need to seek out change, both inward and outward. Longing can make us realize something is missing from our lives and impel us to seek it. Fear can help us see that something is a threat to our well-being.

Ignatius encourages us to give attention to the whole spectrum of our emotional lives, asking ourselves: *Does this emotion expand and deepen my life—or does it make my life narrower, less loving? Can the Spirit of Love use this emotion to teach me something about myself and others?*

When our emotions are "ordered," they empower us to take action, to make changes in our own behaviors and in the structure of our society. This is what Ignatius meant when he said our emotions are the voice of the Spirit. Our emotions tell us: *Look at that. Think about this.*

And then they ask: *What needs to change here?*

Pause

Take a moment to set aside the demands of your busy life. Let yourself rest in the awareness that you are supported and held by the Source, which gives energy to all life. Focus for a moment on your breath as you slowly and consciously exhale and inhale.

When you feel ready, shift your attention from your breath to your emotions. Instead of imagining that emotions are invisible forces living in an intangible part of yourself, picture your emotions as living within your flesh and blood. Scan through your body slowly from head to toe, observing any feelings you find.

You may notice several emotions at work within you, but for now, pick one to focus on. Don't try to identify or label this feeling yet, but instead, imagine yourself holding it gently in your hands, examining it without judgment.

Ask yourself: *How big or small is this feeling? Does it feel heavy or light? Does it have a color? Is it quiet or loud, still or moving? If I could touch this feeling with my hands, how would it feel? What would its texture be?*

Now if you were to give this emotion a label, what would it be? Be precise as possible; don't settle for generic words like "upset" or "happy." Look so closely at this feeling that you can distinguish what makes it different from other emotions.

If you still can't identify your emotion with a sense of clarity, that's okay. Continue to observe it, giving it unconditional acceptance. Simply feel curious—and allow that curiosity to direct your awareness deeper and deeper. If you can't find a single word that identifies what you discover, that's okay too. Try to describe the feeling, using as many words and metaphors as you need. If you feel like it, color a picture, sing, or let your body move as an expression of this feeling.

When you feel comfortable with this emotion, look back at your life over the past few days. Can you recognize ways this emotion shaped your life? Has it been an energizing, life-giving force? Or has it kept you from fully engaging in the circumstances and relationships around you? Has it helped you draw closer to other people? Or has it come between you and others? Does it make your world bigger—or smaller?

As you end this quiet pause, give thanks for all your emotions. Welcome them and love them. Let them know you will not give them control of your life, but you are ready to hear what they are saying—and you will respond with thoughtful action.

5

Conversations
with the Source

On the journey deeper into self-awareness,
I will speak with honesty and gratitude
to the Source of all life.

Words are important. They are among the most basic, the most primal of all the tools we have to make sense of the world. Words shape the way we think—and they shape the way we live.

Words also help to form our connection with Divinity. Even if we don't believe in God in any traditional, religious sense, all of us, particularly in times of need, reach out to something bigger than ourselves. *Please*, our hearts whisper, begging for some form of intervention, some help or deeper understanding. Rather than seeing this as a peaceful and pious interaction, Jungian psychotherapists Ann and Barry Ulanov called prayer a "noisy and vigorous business," which they compared to a baby learning to communicate his needs through screams, wails, sobs, shouts, and whimpers. Prayer, said the Ulanovs, "extends us beyond our known self into the unknown God."

Communication with the Divine is essential to Ignatian spirituality. Ignatius described prayer as an intimate conversation with the One who loves us unconditionally. He called it "colloquy" and described it "as one friend speaks to another . . . now asking some grace, now blaming oneself for some misdeed, now communicating one's affairs, and asking advice."

This concept of prayer creates an opportunity for the Spirit to be expressed in the ever-changing currents of our inner lives. As we practice self-awareness, putting words to our inner thoughts and desires, those words can be an invitation for the Source of life and love to enter our lives. We open ourselves to transformations that take place both internally and externally, both emotionally and behaviorally.

If the thought of conversing with the invisible Source of all life strikes you as presumptuous, silly, or impossible, start here: Look around you. *See* whatever there is to see—a room in your house, a window into the outdoors, a bookshelf, an office desk; notice each detail. Ignatius would tell you that everything you see is in some way a communication from the Divine Spirit. The sun shining through the window, the colors of a painting on the wall, the multihued rows of books on shelves: each whisper, *I'm here . . . and here . . . and here.*

Now extend your gaze; look more closely. See the glint of dust particles in the air. Touch the texture of your chair or a companion animal's fur. Hear the quiet sounds of voices in the distance or the mumbling conversation of your refrigerator and furnace. Pour yourself a cup of coffee or tea, and pay attention to the precise taste in your mouth. Each thing you perceive joins the chorus: *I am here.*

As you go through the rest of your day, look more deeply still. See the despair written on the face of a homeless person, hear the anger at injustice in the voice of an adolescent, feel the physical pain of an older person lying alone in her bed. These too call to you with the Divine Voice:

I am here. See me. Hear me. Touch me. Love me. Answer my voice with your own.

As we stop dividing life into pieces, prayer comes more naturally. We come to see that there is no hazy, invisible "spiritual" reality opposing the "physical" reality we see, hear, touch, taste, and smell. We stop thinking of prayer as religious or supernatural, pertinent only to church-goers and self-labeled "believers." If life were a pie, we realize, we wouldn't be able to cut out a slice of "sacred reality," leaving behind the "secular reality"—because it's all one pie. The physical world is spiritual, and secular reality is sacred. We don't need religion to see that Spirit is everywhere.

Ignatius believed gratitude is the key that opens the door into this vision of reality. Since the Divine Presence is in all things, the life-giving answer to each aspect of our lives is gratitude. Ignatius invites us to pay attention to how love can be found even in the tiniest details of life, but he also challenges us to be attentive and open to how love is at work even in life's sorrow and suffering. Gratitude opens us to seeing the Divine Presence within both the beauty and the mess in our world.

Prayer begins wherever we are. For Ignatius, it began in a sickbed—for us, it might begin during a bout of depression, at a crisis in our marriage, as we face a new responsibility (such as parenthood or a new job), or wherever and whenever we feel pulled out of ourselves, drawn to acknowledge a deeper meaning in our reality. At first, we will bring little to the conversation except for the selfish, chaotic wails of our egos. This form of prayer doesn't need to be censored, though. We don't need to pretend to be more spiritual or more loving than we are. As we express ourselves honestly to the One who loves us unconditionally, we participate in the process of inner transformation. We lay the foundation for living our lives with greater intention and purpose.

Pause

Look back at your day and make a list of the events that stand out to you. Did you notice the sunrise this morning? Did a friend make you laugh? Did the news on the radio, television, or internet fill you with fear or anger?

Consider—what is the Divine Voice saying to you through each of these things? Do you hear the affirmation that you are loved? Or might the Spirit be calling you to take action in some way?

Now respond in words. You may find it easier at first to write rather than speak. If so, write down both sides of a conversation between yourself and God (in whatever form you imagine the Divine—Friend or Lover, Mother or Father, Child or Beast, Tree or Sea . . . or sheer Mystery). Say whatever you want to say to the One who loves you unconditionally—and then imagine you hear responses to your words. Allow your pen to flow across the paper without stopping to edit or criticize your words.

When your pen slows, and you can no longer think of anything to say, stop writing. Read over what you have written. Do you see any new insights about yourself or the Spirit of Love? Does anything surprise you? Does anything make you curious, longing to know more?

Writing this form of prayer may help you feel more comfortable with interacting conversationally with the Unseen—but eventually, you can practice this prayer inside your head, even in the middle of a busy day.

Stage II:

Jesus as a Role Model

6

The Challenge of Love

As I consider the example of Jesus of Nazareth,
I will reflect on how I, too, might be called
to fight suffering and injustice.

In the second stage of the Spiritual Exercises, Ignatius asks us to look at the life of Jesus. However you may feel about Christianity, in either its modern or historical forms— whether you are for or against—I encourage you now to look past the looming shape of organized Christianity. This chapter is not a call to religion, and it doesn't seek to convert you to a particular religious doctrine. Instead, it simply directs your attention toward Jesus of Nazareth, a historical person whose life still has something to say to us today.

As you look at the Jesus portrayed in the Gospels, you will see someone who was an outsider his entire life. According to the Gospel of Luke, Jesus was born in a barn, outside his society's definition of what was acceptable. He came to his own people, but they didn't want him, says the Gospel of John (1:11). You don't need to believe Jesus was literally born in a stable to grasp what the story is saying. Jesus, from the very start, identified with the stranger, the displaced person, the child without a home.

During Jesus's lifetime, his people, the Jews, were under Roman occupation. For nearly a century, they had endured economic exploitation, burdensome taxation, and the lack of autonomy to choose their own course as a nation. Galilee, the region where Jesus grew up, was a boiling cauldron of unrest, always on the point of bubbling over into violence and revolt. When Jesus's friends called him the Messiah, they were expressing their hope that he would be a political savior rather than a spiritual one. They expected him to restore their nation's independence.

They had a hard time grasping Jesus's real purpose. Again and again throughout the Gospels, Jesus expressed his solidarity with people his society had marginalized and ignored. He listened to outsiders and affirmed their identities. He touched people considered to be unclean; he broke the taboos of his people as he had long talks with women; he spent time with people outside his own ethnic group; and even as he was dying, he talked to the man who was on the cross beside him, a man condemned to death for his crimes. According to a later book in the Christian scriptures, Jesus died "outside the city gate"; in his death as in his birth, he was ostracized, pushed outside the acceptable social boundaries.

Although his words and actions repeatedly challenged the governmental and religious authorities, he never, to his followers' great disappointment, made a move to free his people from Roman rule. Instead, he talked a lot about love. He healed people, and he fed them. He told them stories about God and the Divine Realm, he celebrated with them at parties, and he cried with them at funerals. He called people to radical change, a change that had more to do with relationships and the active expression of love than it did with who held political office. He focused on the root causes of our broken world, rather than the symptoms.

This is the Jesus who became the focal point of Ignatius's life. At first, Ignatius often misunderstood Jesus's message;

he battled with his own prejudices, as well as his pride, shame, and quick temper. As he grew more familiar with Jesus, however, he understood him better. (At the same time, Ignatius was also coming to understand himself better.)

Through Jesus's example, Ignatius realized the overlooked people living at the edges of his society had important truths to tell him, truths that insiders—in his day, the knights and nobility, the royalty and the powerful clergy—might never have had the chance to learn. Ignatius saw that people who lack respect and care in our world have often experienced firsthand the meaning of Jesus's life. As they recognize their vulnerability and their dependence on each other, they remind us that our deepest identities do not come from material wealth, education, social status, or physical health. All these things will change and shift throughout our lifetimes. Only love remains the same, holding us steady.

If Jesus is our role model, we can no longer ignore people who are enduring situations we may never have experienced firsthand. When immigrants suffer on our borders, at some level, we all suffer too. The racism that kills young Black men in the streets also kills a part of our own souls. As Indigenous women and girls are missing or murdered, each of our own lives is diminished and threatened. When people are gunned down in supermarkets, churches, and schools, we cannot separate ourselves from their loved ones' pain. And as climate change threatens the water, housing, sanitation, and farmland of millions of people around the world, we must remember we all share the same planet. We cannot claim our own good at the cost of others.

While some religious thought teaches that the "imitation of Christ" is a spiritual, interior activity that requires separation from the world of the senses, Ignatius saw things differently. Just as he saw no difference between the "spiritual" and "physical" realms, he also saw that our inner spiritual lives cannot be severed from our exterior, societal lives. The life of Jesus gave Ignatius a model of inner personal growth embodied in action.

Today, as we see the historical Jesus reach out to heal brokenness and confront injustice, his example continues to challenge us. His life asks us, in effect, to consider and respond to questions like these:

- *Where do you see brokenness?*
- *Where will love take you?*
- *How will your love change the world?*

Pause

Settle yourself for a moment by focusing on your breath. Pay attention to it until your preoccupations with today's circumstances begin to fade.

Then ask yourself these questions:

> *What is my image of Jesus?*
> *What has shaped that image?*
> *Is the Jesus Ignatius came to know the same Jesus I imagine? Why or why not?*

Now think of three characteristics of Jesus that you admire (such as compassion, courage, determination, tolerance, etc.). Ask yourself:

> *How might I express these qualities more fully in my own life?*
> *What stands in the way of me giving these qualities full expression?*

Finally, identify a particular situation in your community, family, or workplace, and ask yourself:

How might I bring one of those three qualities to this situation?

What action could I take that would embody love in these circumstances?

As you leave this pause in your day's activity, carry these questions with you. Rather than seeking to find quick answers, allow these questions to work on your thoughts like yeast in dough, creating and expanding in surprising ways.

7

The Power
of the Imagination

Even as I encounter sorrow and oppression,
both in my life and in the larger world,
I will open myself to the creative powers of my own mind,
asking the Source of infinite love
to bring into being through me
new ideas, new realities, new possibilities.

Ignatius was one of those people naturally gifted with a powerful imagination. During his long convalescence after his battle injury, his long daydreams about romance and glory helped him pass the time. He imagined himself dressed in stylish clothes, admired by everyone he met. He pictured himself as a courageous knight, winning death-defying duels that would win him fame and honor.

Then, after reading a book about the lives of the saints, he also began to daydream about walking in the saints' footsteps, living his life the way they had lived theirs. In the weeks that followed, lying in his bed, he went back and forth between these fantasies. Through his imagination, he tried out differing life directions—and he came to some realizations.

While his daydreams about romantic intrigues, battle glory, and fashionable society attracted him, seeming to promise him pleasure and satisfaction, he noticed they left behind an unsettling feeling of anxiety. However, as he used his imagination to enter into the saints' lives, he found himself feeling comforted and encouraged. As his heart and emotions responded to these fantasies, he heard the Divine Voice drawing him toward a new way of life.

For Ignatius, the imagination—what psychologists today define as the ability to form a mental image of something not currently perceived through the five senses—was not limited to a visual "picture" he held in the mind; Ignatius discovered that the imagination is even more powerful when it incorporates all our senses and emotions. While today we often dismiss the products of our imagination as delusions or childish make-believe, Ignatius came to believe the imagination is a faculty that allows us to interact with the world at a deeper level. Although he recognized that we are often prone to using our imaginations to stroke our egos, as he had done with his daydreams about romance and fame, he also saw that the imagination can be an effective vehicle for spiritual growth.

Modern scientific research is confirming Ignatius's beliefs about the imagination. It turns out that from a neurological perspective, we perceive imaginary scenarios as if they were "real." This means we can use our imaginations to overcome our fears about certain things or situations; as we imagine ourselves encountering these fear-inspiring people, places, things, or activities, we gain familiarity with them—and that familiarity also may provide an antidote for anxiety.

Among those positive gifts imagination provides is that it fuels empathy, allowing us to explore what it means to feel, see, and think as another person. We can also use our imagination to develop and practice physical skills. Coaches have found that athletic performance depends as much on mental (imaginary) "practice" as it does on physical preparation. If you are learning to play the piano, and you imagine yourself practicing scales, you build neural connections that allow your fingers to perform better the next time you sit down to play. Psychologists are even finding we can "update" troubling memories by using our imagination to insert healing elements into memories that may have been putting unnecessary limits on our lives. Ignatius recommended placing Jesus and Divine love into the story; psychologists today would recommend retelling a painful memory in any way that empowers us. The imagination allows us to take steps toward healing.

Ignatius emphasized that the imagination is also a powerful lens into the life of Jesus. Put yourself there at the newborn's manger, Ignatius said. Imagine the smell of the animals and the afterbirth. See the lamplight as it shines on the mother and child. Hear the soft noises a newborn makes. Feel the texture of the straw. Taste the dust and the dirt on your tongue. And then let yourself respond emotionally. *Be fully present with Jesus.*

We cannot see the Divine with our physical eyes or touch Divinity with our fingers—but our imagination allows us to experience a wider and deeper reality than our five senses can perceive. It allows us, Ignatius taught, to engage more fully with the Spirit of Love. Imagination brings new life to our otherwise dry, emotionless ideas about God. It allows us to interact with the Source of life, offering us a vehicle for a steady practice of prayer.

The imagination not only empowers our spiritual and emotional growth; by its light, we also envision ways to bring growth to the world around us. In a world of limitation and frustration, the imagination shows us innovative ways forward toward freedom and fulfillment. It enables us to build something altogether new. Think about people like Grace Hopper and Steve Jobs; their imaginations contributed to the development of computers that changed the way we live. Because people like them (and many others) had the courage and creativity to imagine the unknown, today we entertain ourselves, educate ourselves, do our work, and communicate with each other in ways our ancestors would never have dreamed possible.

When we look at our world, we see war and violence, prejudice and hatred, and yet, through the unlimited vision of the human imagination—the capacity to create mental pictures of things that don't yet exist—each circumstance of our lives becomes an opportunity for new life to emerge. Through our imaginations, we discover ways to build bridges, to heal and restore, to include and affirm. We see how to make the unconditional love of Divinity come alive, both in our hearts and in our world.

Pause

Take a few moments to quiet your mind and body. Focus on your breathing—and then shift your attention to an awareness that includes both your physical and emotional sensations. Recognize each of these one by one—but then let them go, rather than allowing them to capture your attention.

Now imagine yourself walking with Jesus of Nazareth. Build the scene with sensory details: *What does Jesus look like? What is he wearing? What is his expression? Where are you and he walking? What does the road or path look like? What do you hear, smell, taste, and feel?*

Once you have this scene clear in your mind, turn to Jesus (in your imagination), and begin to talk to him.

Tell him anything that is weighing on your mind. Feel free to ask him questions—and allow your imagination to "hear" and supply the answers. If you find your mind wandering, consider putting this imaginary conversation into writing. The psychoanalyst Carl Jung, who recommended a similar practice he called *active imagination*, encouraged writing as a way to keep our imagination focused.

When you are ready to leave your conversation, take a few moments to bring your thoughts back into your ordinary life. Reflect on any realization that came to you through your time with Jesus.

8

Heart's Desire

Seeking to expand my self-awareness,
I let go of any disguises I have learned to hide behind,
so I can identify my truest and deepest longings.

The religious life is often seen as a life of self-denial. For many of us, this image holds little appeal. What emotionally healthy person would choose to give up everything that gives them pleasure? Ignatius, however, looked at Jesus and saw past the restriction of religion. Instead, in the life of Jesus, Ignatius found affirmation of his heart's deepest longings.

But before he came to that understanding, Ignatius needed to pull away the outer shells he'd built around his true core. During the early months of his conversion, he ruthlessly examined his life and determined which aspects of himself brought him no real joy. His need for romantic conquests, his love of fancy clothes, his desire for glory on the battlefield—all these, he realized, were empty shells he'd built to hide behind. None of them satisfied the deepest yearnings of his heart.

Stripped of the disguises he'd been wearing, he now stood naked in his most essential self. He returned to a state of being from an earlier time when he had not yet learned to be anything but what and who he was. As Ignatius let go of his outer dignity, he recovered the primordial integrity that had been his all along. He became like a child.

The Gospels describe Jesus interacting with children, and portrayals of Jesus surrounded by children have become standard religious art. We may take for granted that Jesus would have, of course, valued kids. Embedded as we are in a culture that values children and childhood, we fail to see that when Jesus gathered children around him, he was, as he did so often, making a statement that countered the assumptions of his society.

Children in Jesus's day had very little societal worth. More than half of the children born at the time never

reached puberty. Knowing this, adults may have held themselves emotionally separate from children. In a culture dom-
inated by adult men, children held the lowest social status of
anyone. Their needs, let alone their rights, were not priori-
tized. Caring for children was the responsibility of women,
another group of people who lacked status or power in the
first century. A man might be affectionate to his own children in his home, but in the regular course of life, he would
never be seen hugging them or engaging with children in
public.

And so, when Jesus made a point of interacting with
children, he wasn't just being a warm-hearted man showing
off his feminine side. He was making a far more subversive
statement. In the Gospels, he tells his friends and followers to welcome children, telling us still today that no one—
no child, no person—is outside the circle of Divine love.
Everyone—even the people society considers expendable,
the people we may even forget altogether—has a place of
honor within God's embrace.

But then Jesus goes still further. Not only are children included and valued by Divine love, but children, says
Jesus, know far more than adults about what he called the
realm of heaven. In saying this, Jesus radically challenges

the accepted norms for power and privilege and piety. "Whoever welcomes a child," he says, "welcomes me—the embodiment of Divine love." In other words, each new child who enters the world brings Divinity with them.

This is the obscured identity we each carry within us. It is the essence of who we really are. As we strip away all that has hidden and suppressed our true selfdom, we encounter our child-selves. We gain access to our deepest, most essential yearnings.

What does a child desire? Children are not immune to our materialistic culture, of course—as they grow older, they feel the appeal of acquisition just as much as adults do—but before they are exposed to advertising, before they learn to compare their possessions to their friends', all children desire and need certain elemental things.

Beyond children's most basic needs for food and safety, all children need love. They need the experience of being in loving relationships where they not only receive love but learn to express it as well. They also need opportunities to learn, to express their curiosity and find answers. As they grow older, they require opportunities to take the initiative and contribute to their world. As they gain a sense of their own inner authority and creativity, they find ways to actively express these. They know their lives have value.

When we dare stand naked in our childlike vulnerability, with all our pretenses stripped away, we realize these are the same things we still need as adults. Each of us yearns for love, for meaning, for opportunities to contribute our unique skills and resources to the larger world. Based on Ignatius's own experience as he grew spiritually, he invites us to examine and clarify these most authentic and deep-seated desires in our own lives.

Longing expresses our sense that something is needed in our lives, something that is essential to our happiness and well-being. Ignatius believed that when we identify our truest desires—the deep yearnings of our souls rather than the more shallow wishes we've absorbed from our society—there will be no conflict between what we want and what God wants because our yearning hearts naturally point us to the Source of life.

Not only are satisfaction and fulfillment essential to us growing into our most complete selves, but our own desires meet and merge with the Divine desire for love, for justice, for a world where people are valued and affirmed. Ultimately, Ignatius believed, what we desire is also the Divine call on our lives. As we respond, each in our own individual way, we find interior fulfillment, even as we build a better world.

Pause

As you pause from your life's demands, allow yourself a few moments to calm and settle your thoughts. Again, focusing on your breathing is an easy way to do this, but you may also choose another focus, such as music. Candles are often used as visual focal points, and incense may serve as an olfactory focus. During the small spaces of calm offered in the remaining chapters of this book, experiment with what works best to bring you a centered sense of quiet.

Now, once again, use your imagination as a tool for spiritual deepening. Picture yourself first as a child. Remember with as much detail as you can what it felt like to be very young. Consciously let go of your adult ideas about your identity and settle into this much smaller version of yourself.

Once you have gotten in touch with your child-self, next imagine an encounter with Jesus. Picture the scene as clearly as you can. What is Jesus doing? Where is he? What does the setting look like? (Are you outside or indoors? Are you in the woods or by the sea, in your childhood living room or at your grandmother's house? Imagine a location where you feel completely safe.) What does Jesus look like? What do you feel as you approach him? Do you feel shy, happy, afraid, angry? Feel free to acknowledge any emotion honestly.

Now, whether on paper or in your imagination, have a conversation with Jesus. Talk to him about what you yearn for most. Again, be honest. There are no right or wrong answers. Simply let your childhood self speak from the heart.

When you have fully expressed yourself, take a moment to listen for anything Jesus says to you in return. Do not try to force him to conform to your image of how Jesus should act or talk. Allow your imagination to know more than your conscious mind does. Open yourself to surprise.

When you are ready to leave your conversation, take a few moments to bring your thoughts back into your ordinary life. Reflect on any realization that came to you through your time as a child with Jesus.

9

Decision-Making

As I become more aware of my emotions and desires,
I use them as though they were a compass,
pointing me in the direction I need to go.

Ignatian spirituality is sometimes seen as a process of decision-making. Ignatius called this process "discernment." His understanding of discernment was based on his belief that the Divine Spirit is constantly at work in our lives, guiding us into a way of life rooted in love.

The English word *discernment* comes from a Latin word meaning "to sift or separate." Ignatius's process of discernment is a method by which we separate constructive, life-giving actions from ones that are destructive and death-dealing. This process relies on the self-awareness he emphasized in the first stage of his Spiritual Exercises, as well as relies on our ability to be in touch with our own emotions. It also requires an alert openness to circumstances we observe in the world around us.

Ignatius asks us to consider:

What do I want to say yes to?
And what do I want to say no to?

He encourages us not to answer these questions quickly or automatically, and not to rely on any form of outside pressure or assumptions. Instead, he offers us a decision-making process to determine how our unique voices will be heard in the world: how we can align our specific gifts and heart-yearnings with what the world around us most needs.

This is not an intellectual exercise so much as a practice of deep spiritual consciousness. To find the way of life and love, Ignatius taught, we "must first of all put aside all affection and preference for one thing rather than another." Once we have detached ourselves from any bias, we pay close attention to our feelings. As we become more fully aware of these internal movements of our souls and the desires that drive them, we begin to hear the voice of Love speaking through the pendulum swing of our emotional lives.

Ignatius believed our emotions offer us either *consolation* or *desolation*. He used this dichotomy not to separate what we would consider positive emotions (happiness, gratitude, peace, hope, and so on) from negative ones (such as anger, fear, sadness, guilt) but rather to distinguish between emotions that drive us closer to love and those that pull us away from love.

Consolation, in this sense, energizes us to reach out in love; we feel encouraged and empowered, connected to the Source of life, as well as to other human beings and the entire cosmic world. Consolation brings a sense of freedom and rightness. It opens our hearts so we feel greater compassion for others, and it inspires us to actively work for justice and inclusion.

Desolation, on the other hand, brings confusion and anxiety. It makes us feel cut off from the living universe, trapped within our narrow viewpoints, preoccupied with our selfish fears and urges. As our egos shout for recognition and control, they give us no peace or sense of fulfillment;

instead, they drive us with an urgent sense of desperation, a constant restless seeking for pleasure and power.

By paying attention to the differences between these two emotional forces, Ignatius taught, we learn to navigate our way more wisely through life's many choices.

Ignatius believed his process of discernment should not be reserved only for momentous, life-changing decisions (such as choosing a life partner, changing professions, or moving across the country). Even though circumstances like these may lead to our first realization that we need a tool for decision-making, it's in the practice of the process in all our different circumstances that we become more comfortable with it. After enough repetition, it becomes habitual to apply Ignatian discernment even to the countless, seemingly trivial decisions we encounter every day. We allow discernment to guide us regarding how we make use of the physical world, the people we connect with, and the projects we take on. Discernment becomes a daily, repetitive process that allows us to fine-tune our choices to better align with our innermost selves—and to course-correct when we find ourselves lost.

Ignatian discernment is not merely a spiritual way of drawing straws, and it's not a magic formula that ensures we find the one and only path to what is best for us. It's not so much about reaching our predestined destination as it is about the paths we take to reach that destination. Think of it like driving a car: those constant, almost imperceptible adjustments of the wheel are very much like the lifelong practice of discernment.

Ignatius acknowledged that discernment can lack clarity. Sometimes, we're faced with two options that both lead in positive directions. In those cases, Ignatius taught, we look for whatever leads to the fullest and most far-reaching expression of love. Ignatius also recognized that the need for absolute certainty can be paralyzing, preventing us from moving forward in any direction. On one occasion, he himself fell into "desolation" because he could not clearly see the precise path he should take. He realized, finally, that his desire for absolute certainty on a direction was actually a desire for control; he didn't want to risk making a mistake that might lead to failure. Once he realized this and released his ego's need to be in charge, he stepped out on a path forward, even though he could not yet see the outcome of his decision.

The process of discernment, Ignatius understood, requires humility. It asks that we be willing to let go of ego and risk making mistakes, knowing the Source of life will be with us in the process, even through what we perceive as our failures.

Pause

Once again, this is a chance to step back from your busy life. Spend a few moments letting go of all the concerns that have preoccupied you today. You can pick them up later—they won't go anywhere—but for now, set them aside. Focus on your breath, listen to music, gaze at a candle or out the window, burn incense, or simply breathe the breeze that comes in through an open window. Do whatever helps you to quiet your mind and find a moment of peace. Let yourself rest in this moment for as long as you need to.

When you are ready, picture another scene from the life of Jesus. This time, imagine you see the adolescent Jesus as his parents take him to the temple and he begins to talk with the rabbis there. See how happy he looks as he sits there, asking and answering questions with men three times his age. Notice the men's robes, their long beards, the fringes on their cloaks.

Now imagine you can also see Jesus's parents, Mary and Joseph, who discover Jesus is missing from their large group traveling together. They don't know where their son has gone. Picture them as they search for him through the crowded streets of Jerusalem, hear the growing fear in their voices, and let their anxiety fill your own heart. For a parent, losing a child is one of the most terrifying experiences.

Watch as Mary and Joseph are reunited with Jesus. Hear the exasperation, even anger, in their voices as they scold him for wandering off on his own.

Next, imagine yourself sitting down with Jesus and Mary and Joseph to discuss what happened. Listen to what Joseph and Mary have to say—and then ask Jesus to tell his perspective. According to this story as it's told in the second chapter of the Gospel of Luke, Jesus told his parents he was listening to God's voice, following Divine direction rather than his parents'.

When Jesus has finished speaking, ask him if he used a process like Ignatian discernment when he decided to go off by himself. What does he answer? Imagine how he describes both the "consolation" and the "desolation" he experienced as he made his choice.

At first glance, we might assume that Jesus's priority as a young person was to comply with his parents' expectations. Jesus, however, saw past this cultural assumption and answered a deeper call that came from his inner self. Consider for a few moments: *Are there any societal assumptions that are holding you back from hearing the call of your deepest heart's desire? Can you separate your desire to go along with what's expected of you from your desire for a wider, more inclusive life?*

As you return to the rest of your day, carry these questions with you. Be open to discovering new directions for your life.

10

Friendship and Community

Because I seek to grow as a spiritual being,
I will nourish and protect my relationships with others,
working to build a healthier world for us all.

People sometimes think of Ignatian spirituality as a path to individualism. But despite Ignatius's emphasis on interior self-examination, his focus on Jesus inspired him to reach out beyond himself. As he saw Divinity in the faces of everyone he encountered, he came to understand that the good of each individual is ultimately dependent on the good of everyone. His interior spiritual growth expressed itself in a network of relationship with others. As he contributed his own life and energy to this lattice of connection and commitment, it supported and nurtured him in return.

As modern-day Westerners, many of us have lost sight of what Indigenous cultures have never forgotten: we all exist within a living network, a breathing, growing web of intertwined life. The Christian scriptures sometimes refer to this with the metaphor of a body, in which all the organs, limbs, and senses are essential not only to the overall well-being of the larger organism but also to its individual parts. What is good for the toe is good for the heart as well, and what damages the lungs also causes irritation to the skin.

This holistic perspective is contrary not only to our modern model for medical treatment but also to our understanding of how the entire world works. We've been taught that fierce competition is the road to success; I achieve my success by defeating you, while you attain your goals by being better than me. We assume humans have priority over other life-forms, and we may even believe our nation's triumph is worth another country's destruction. We fail to see through these delusions to the reality. We cannot untangle our well-being from that of all the other lives with whom we share our planet. Our well-being is so interwoven that "rugged individualism" makes no sense—neither in spiritual terms, as we commit ourselves to the demands of love, nor in practical terms, where that love is lived in action. As conservationist Julian Hoffman wrote, "Given that everything on this planet is interwoven, and each interaction . . . affects others further down the line, the only way to credibly care for human health is to consider all the pieces" of our shared world, all those big and small pieces that are constantly interacting.

In the life of Jesus, Ignatius saw a model for the kind of relationships that support our interconnected world. Friendships built on respect and self-giving love were essential to Ignatius's understanding of how the Divine intercedes in and influences human life. These are not the sort of friendships that generate exclusion, the cliquishness of in-groups and out-groups; they are instead the human embodiment of God's unconditional love. Ignatius believed God calls us to extend this attitude of friendship and acceptance to all human beings, regardless of their societal status.

Ignatius's concept of intentional relationship was built on always desiring the greater good for one another. Committed friendship then becomes the substructure of our communal lives, a mesh of relationships that holds us and sustains us. In each other's faces, we see the Spirit of Love embodied—and as we respond with reciprocal acceptance and commitment, we too enter the flow of Divine life.

This sacred life takes form in many ways. One that Ignatius pointed out in particular is being "patient in listening to all people." As we let go of our preoccupations and defenses, as we stop trying to protect and inflate our own egos, we become able to hear more accurately what others are saying.

Ignatius wrote that those who follow the example of Jesus "must be disposed to receive in a favorable sense and to take in good part every word susceptible of being so received and understood, rather than to take it in a rigorous and objectionable sense." In other words, we listen not so we can argue or find fault but so that we can better understand a different perspective from our own. Rather than listening through the filter of our own assumptions or leaping to false conclusions, by listening in the spirit of friendship and keeping a receptive posture, we are "more ready to justify than to condemn."

This form of active listening helps to build bridges that allow communication and mutual enrichment to cross back and forth between us. It leads to the reconciliation our divided world so badly needs. This doesn't mean, however, that all our differences disappear. Instead, reconciliation affirms that differences are real and to be respected. If you and I were exactly the same, there would be nothing we could learn from each other. But because we are different from one another, we each offer our own weird and wonderful qualities that enhance and fortify each other's lives. Together, we work to create harmony based on respecting and valuing each other's unique qualities rather than eradicating them.

The Spiritual Exercises challenge us to see all reality as participating in an animate and sacred unity. Each element of our world, including the social aspects of living within a society made up of other human beings, has the potential to come together in conscious and loving union. This vision creates a spirituality far more all-encompassing than the narrow focus of a purely me-and-God outlook. Ignatius calls us to a spirituality expressed by the fabric of God, community, and me, a spirituality of conscious commitment that stretches out to include all humanity, as well as animal and plant life and the Earth itself.

Our spiritual lives are not based on navel-gazing. Instead, our interior journeys lead us back into the exterior world, where we are called to practice intentional love. Through our inner work, we gain the consciousness we need to step free of the selfishness that damages and severs our relationships. We look past the narrow scope of what we think of as our personal interests, and we commit ourselves to a larger communal well-being that spreads and grows, working to heal our broken world.

Pause

Take a few moments to quiet your mind. Breathe in, breathe out. Consciously relax your muscles, starting with your toes and working your way upward to your neck, face, and scalp.

When you feel quiet and settled, call to mind a time when you had difficulty interacting with another person. Identify the emotions you felt at the time, whether anger, hurt, frustration, or even disgust. Did your emotions focus on your inability to understand—or on the other person's failure to listen? What judgments, assumptions, or beliefs fueled your reactions? Did you express your feelings? How did the interaction end? How do you feel now as you remember it?

Now consider how Jesus interacted with others. He was consistently gentle and respectful as he reached out to people who lived on the margins of his society, including women, children, and people with chronic illnesses—but he could also be outspoken, even angry, when he confronted power that was oppressive or unjust.

Either on paper or only in your imagination, create a conversation with Jesus about the interaction on which you just reflected. Be honest and open about your feelings. Speak with him about any feelings you have of alienation or loneliness, anger or judgment—and then consider any ways in which you erect or contribute to barriers between yourself and others. Is there anything Jesus points out to you?

As you bring these quiet moments to an end and return to the demands of your life, carry with you an increased sensitivity to your interactions with family members, work colleagues, and community contacts. Notice what behaviors and words contribute to understanding and harmony—and what hinder relationships and create division.

Stage III:

Suffering and Death

11

Solidarity with Those Who Suffer

As I consider those who suffer in our world,
I look for ways to identify with them,
so that I may see and participate
in the Divine life present in each person.

In this third stage of the Spiritual Exercises, Ignatius asks us to focus on the pain and death Jesus experienced at the end of his life on Earth. This need not be a purely spiritual exercise; we also have the option of experiencing for ourselves Jesus's solidarity with those who are suffering. In doing so, we come to a new understanding of suffering and death.

Christianity has often preached that Jesus had no interest in politics, that his mission was purely "religious," focused on the spiritual rather than social world. When we look at Jesus's words and actions in the Gospels, however, we see a person whose entire life was about politics, in the sense that politics has to do with how power is used. Jesus never mentioned setting up a new religion in his name; what he did talk about constantly was empowering the power-less. Again and again, he described a community where all are welcomed and included, where healing and affirmation rather than exploitation and debasement are the goals of all relationships.

In the Gospels, Jesus often uses stories and metaphors to help his listeners understand his message. Jesus under-stood that imagination is a powerful spiritual faculty, some-thing that Ignatius would also be compelled by many years later. The Gospel of Matthew records this story Jesus told his followers about a Divine Host who greets humanity at the end of time, saying:

"Come . . . inherit the world prepared for you since the creation of the universe. For I was hungry, and you fed me. I was thirsty, and you gave me a drink. I was a stranger, and you invited me into your home. I was naked, and you gave me clothing. I was sick, and you cared for me. I was in prison, and you visited me."

Then, these humans who did whatever they could to care for others will say to the Host:

"When did we ever see you hungry and feed you? Or thirsty and give you something to drink? Or a stranger and show you hospitality? Or naked and give you clothing? When did we ever see you sick or in prison and visit you?"

And the Host will say, "I tell you the truth, when you did it to one of the least of these my brothers and sisters, you were doing it to me!"

As Jesus's story continues, the Host talks to another group of people whose goal in life was the satisfaction of their selfishness. To this group of people, the Host says:

"I was hungry, and you didn't feed me. I was thirsty, and you didn't give me a drink. I was a stranger, and you didn't invite me into your home. I was naked, and you didn't give me clothing. I was sick and in prison, and you didn't visit me."

The people protest: "When did we ever see you hungry or thirsty or a stranger or naked or sick or in prison, and not help you?"

And the Host answers: "I tell you the truth, when you refused to help the least of these my brothers and sisters, you were refusing to help me."

Theologian and author Kelly Brown Douglas suggests that in our world today, the question we ask Jesus (assuming he is the Host in the story) might be: "When did we see you dying, murdered by injustice?"

And Jesus will answer: "On a sidewalk, at a gas station, in back yards and parking lots where police gunned down innocent Black folk. As you did it to one of these young Black bodies, you did it to me."

Jesus might also say we abandoned him on our borders and in our nursing homes; we allowed him to suffer from malnourishment and inadequate medical care; and we imprisoned him along with other people with brown and black skin. We failed to see the presence of Divinity in the woman talking to herself on the street corner, in the child and his mother sleeping under newspapers in a doorway, and in the teenager shooting drugs under a bridge. Each human being is sacred, Jesus taught. And as Ignatius came to understand this, he too, like Jesus, identified himself with those his society had forgotten or oppressed.

The Spiritual Exercises call us to also align ourselves in solidarity with all who are marginalized, who suffer from a society that does not support or welcome them. This solidarity doesn't mean uniformity, a unity where all distinctions melt and run together. It also doesn't mean offering condescending charity to the "less fortunate." Father Greg Boyle, a Jesuit priest who works with inner-city gangs, wrote that solidarity "lies less in our service of those on the margins, and more in our willingness to see ourselves in kinship with them. It speaks of a kinship so mutually rich that even the dividing line of service provider/service recipient is erased."

People often ask the question, "Why does God allow suffering?" Ignatius challenges us to remember that it is we humans who, directly or indirectly, cause suffering. The Source of all life is present, however, with those who suffer, and, according to the Gospels, Jesus also suffers with them.

As we follow in Ignatius's and Jesus's footsteps, we too will see and honor the Divine image in each suffering individual. Then, empowered by the Divine Host, we will stretch out our arms in welcome as we work to put right each situation that causes human pain.

Pause

Again, take advantage of this pause in your day. Let tension flow out of you with each exhalation. Allow a sense of peace to flow into you with each inhalation. Breathe in peace, breathe out tension, until you feel quiet, in your body, your mind, and your spirit.

Now turn your thoughts to the story Jesus told about the Host. Either on paper or totally in your imagination, have a conversation with Jesus about why he told this story. Listen and reflect on what he says to you. Ask him to point out any times you have overlooked the Divine image in the people with whom you interact.

As these quiet moments come to an end, carry them at the background of your mind as you go about the rest of your day. Return to them whenever you can. Consciously seek to see the image of God in all people, especially those who are going through suffering and hardship.

12

The Call

As I open my heart to hearing the call of justice,
I will align my heart and my actions
with those who are oppressed.

In another story Jesus tells in the Gospels, he describes a man who has been assaulted and now lies wounded next to the road. Various religious leaders pass the man; they see him, but they do not stop. Instead, they avert their gaze and stay on their own side of the road, in order to avoid glimpsing the ugliness and agony of violence. Like so many of us, these men didn't want to risk getting involved.

But then, Jesus says, a person from a despised minority group comes along. Unlike the powerful and religious people who refused to interrupt their journeys, this person leaves her path and gets down in the ditch with the man. She bandages his wounds, and then, paying for all his expenses, she takes him somewhere he can heal in safety and comfort.

"Which of these people was a good neighbor to the wounded man?" Jesus asks as he finishes his story.

Jesus told this story in response to a question from a religious person who asked him how to find everlasting life. Jesus first pointed him back to the ancient Hebrew scriptures, which say, "Love God with all your heart, all your soul, all your strength, and all your mind—and love your neighbor as yourself."

"But who is my neighbor?" the religious man asked Jesus. Just as we do so often, the man was looking for wiggle room, a way to excuse his failure to respond to love's call. If our neighbors are the people who live near us geographically, then we are excused from caring about suffering that happens outside our own community. Like the religious men in Jesus's story, we can go on with our lives, never allowing ourselves to see the wider implications of suffering.

But Jesus's story tells us that our neighbor—the person we are called to love as much as we love ourselves—is anyone who suffers, anyone who needs our help and intervention. Wherever suffering exists, there we hear the Divine call to become involved, to take action on behalf of others. This is the call Ignatius heard as well.

The call to action applies in many practical ways to our current world—for example, racism. Clinical psychologist Beverly Tatum has suggested there are four levels of racial identity among white people, the first being the actively racist white supremacist; in Jesus's story, we might say this was the person who attacked and wounded the man by the road. Tatum's second level is someone who refuses to acknowledge either racism or the fact that whites have privileges denied to people of color; we can compare this person to the religious leaders who went on their way without looking at the wounded man. Tatum's third category is the guilty white person, someone who is aware of racism and feels bad about it; this could be equated to someone Jesus might easily have included in his story, someone who saw the wounded man, felt terrible, and then went on her way, haunted by guilt. Finally, the fourth level of racial identity is someone who actively becomes an ally with people of color, someone who makes a commitment to recognize his own privilege, and then works in solidarity with people of color in the struggle for justice.

Many of us probably find ourselves in Tatum's two middle categories. We would never actively harm a person of color, but we either ignore the issue of racism altogether or feel guilty but fail to take any action. Research psychologist Janet Helms reports studies indicating that about half of all white people are indifferent to the issues that impact people of color. It's not that they wish anyone harm, but when it comes right down to it, they simply don't care one way or another. As Holocaust survivor and author Elie Wiesel once said, "The opposite of love is not hate, it's indifference."

Our defensive egos find ways to excuse or justify our refusal to answer justice's call. In this case, we may talk about reverse racism, refusing to see the institutionalized privilege even the poorest whites carry. Or we say the problem is too big, too complicated and overwhelming for us to begin to know how to take action. Besides, we already have plenty of responsibilities; we're too busy and too tired to add one more thing to our crowded schedules.

Oscar Romero, who gave his life for the cause of justice in El Salvador, had answers for these excuses. "I don't want to be an anti, against anyone. I simply want to be a builder of a great affirmation." He recognized that in our interwoven world, as we affirm others, we too are affirmed; as we fight for others' freedom, we too are freed. Romero also acknowledged, "We cannot do everything," but he went on to say, "there is a sense of liberation in realizing that. This enables us to do something, and to do it very well. It may be incomplete, but it is a beginning, a step along the way." Dorothy Day, another activist-theologian, affirmed the same message: "People say, what is the sense of our small effort? They cannot see that we must lay one brick at a time, take one step at a time. A pebble cast into a pond causes ripples that spread in all directions. Each one of our thoughts, words and deeds is like that. No one has a right to sit down and feel hopeless. There is too much work to do." Romero and Day believed that when we lay that first brick or take that first step, we create an opening for the Spirit of Love to enter our world, magnifying our small efforts and shining light on a path forward.

Yet another activist-theologian, Gustavo Gutiérrez, reminds us to be wise and far-seeing as we respond to the call for justice. Our individual actions may be small, but we need to focus them on the real problems, not just the symptoms. "The poverty of the poor," Gutiérrez says, "is not a call to generous relief action, but a demand that we go and build a different social order." This is the call Jesus answered. It is the one that shaped Ignatius's life as well. And it is the same call that beckons us out of our indifference and defensiveness, into a life of radical and active love.

The call of justice isn't about finding ways to be comfortable with our guilt. It's not about redeeming ourselves or becoming good people or impressing others with our compassion. In fact, it's not about us at all. Instead, it summons us to real and practical solidarity with people who are suffering and oppressed. "The ones who have a voice," said Oscar Romero, "must speak for those who are voiceless."

Pause

Take a few moments to breathe in peace and breathe out tension, allowing your body to relax as your thoughts quiet and settle. If your thoughts wander during this small pause in your day, return your attention to your breath until you are once more focused and calm.

Now reflect on this question: *When I witness injustice, what gets in the way of me taking action in response?* Think of as many things as you can. Identify each inner or outer barrier, without defensiveness or shame. Simply see each thing that interferes with you answering the larger call of love.

Next, take two or three items from your list and allow yourself to become aware of the thoughts, emotions, or body sensations that arise as you reflect on each one. Look at these feelings with an attitude of curiosity, opening yourself to the desire to learn more. Ask yourself: *How are these reactions getting in the way of me taking action on behalf of others?*

Picture each inner barrier within you as a physical obstacle. Imagine yourself picking up each one and removing it from your path. What does your path forward look like now? With these obstacles removed, what can you imagine doing?

When you leave this quiet time, continue to reflect on these questions. Come back to them throughout your day, and allow them to expand within you, creating new space and possibilities within you and around you.

13

Humility

I will cultivate a realistic perspective of my own skills and weaknesses, opening my heart and mind to the joy of learning new ideas and possibilities that challenge my assumptions.

Justice calls us to live in solidarity with those who are oppressed or suffering—but actually doing so requires humility. It asks us to let go of any belief in our own superiority. Regardless of how educated or intelligent we are, how many privileges we take for granted, and how many talents and other resources we have to offer, Jesus reminds us in the Gospels to be like children: curious, eager to learn, vulnerable in our love.

This is similar to what Buddhists call "beginner's mind." The more we know about something, the more closed our minds often become to learning more. We make assumptions based on our current knowledge, and we no longer leave room for curiosity and surprise. The child-like mind—the beginner's mind—has the humility needed to learn. Humility and curiosity walk hand in hand, leading to a life of joy and wonder.

In the Spiritual Exercises, Ignatius analyzes three levels of humility:

- At the first level, we recognize we are neither the center of the world nor the ruler of it; we see our place in the world realistically, without the inflation of pride and ego.
- At the second level, we surrender our attachments to exterior things; we no longer rely on our material possessions, our skills, or our reputations for our identities.
- At the third level, we achieve total identification with Jesus.

All three levels of humility are good—each is a step forward on love's path—but the "greater good" (a term that describes Ignatius's constant goal) is the third level. There, as we model our lives on Jesus's example in the Gospels, we not only surrender our egos' demands for recognition and control, but we also allow love to constantly and consistently guide the shape of our lives. We do not dwell on guilt or self-hate because we have no need of either. More occupied with others' reality than our own, we no longer have any need to prove ourselves. We are so open to learning, to new understanding, that we begin to see possibilities we had never previously considered.

Ignatius challenges us to consider: *What does this aspect of the Spiritual Exercises say to us today? What does it say to those of us who are within the Christian tradition? What does it say to those who are from other spiritual traditions? Is Ignatius calling us to religious conversion? Or does Ignatius's analysis of humility ultimately point us toward a way of life open to anyone, regardless of religious beliefs? Can anyone who seeks the common good find it in Jesus's example in the Gospels?*

At first glance, humility may not seem to be an appealing trait, nor even a particularly helpful one in our modern world. The word *humility* comes from the root word *humus*, meaning earth or soil. Why would we want to identify ourselves with *dirt*? The very thought of it clashes with our ideas about self-esteem and self-realization.

But humility doesn't ask us to be weak, self-effacing, or submissive. If we look at the stories of Jesus confronting authority, we see that his humility led him to courage and action, rather than silence and invisibility. Nor does humility mean we spend all our time thinking about our own faults and guilt; ironically, a negative preoccupation with our failures can be a form of narcissism, focusing our attention on ourselves rather than others. Ignatius said pride is the "fuel" that feeds guilt and self-hatred, and in the sixteenth century, Francis de Sales, who trained in Ignatian spirituality, wrote about people who "decline to use their talents in the service of God and their neighbor, because, forsooth, they know their weakness, and are afraid of becoming proud if they do any good thing." Francis concluded that this is "not merely a spurious but a vicious humility" that asks us to create an unreal picture of ourselves and our world; it "tacitly and secretly condemns God's gifts, and makes a pretext of lowliness while really exalting self-love, self-sufficiency, indolence, and evil tempers."

True humility lets go of the lies (both the positive ones and the negative) we've told ourselves about our own selves.

Humility no longer sees the self as having an exaggerated importance. Jesus's humility was based on not taking his own desires, successes, or failings too seriously—an attitude that generated a life of active love.

The American Psychological Association defines humility as a "low focus on the self, an accurate (not over- or underestimated) sense of one's accomplishments and worth, and an acknowledgment of one's limitations, imperfections, mistakes, gaps in knowledge, and so on." Because humility requires that we cultivate a mindset that embraces constant self-correction and self-improvement, psychological research indicates that it has positive effects on our abilities to analyze, reflect, and make good decisions, as well as our social skills. Humble people are better learners and problem solvers; they get out of their own way so that they more effectively utilize the resources they find both within themselves and in the outer world. Some studies have even found that humility is more important as an indicator of future performance than a high score on an intelligence test.

Ignatius was action-oriented, focused far more on feelings and behaviors than on beliefs, but at the same time, he also encouraged a shift in attention, away from the need to prove worth through visible achievements and instead toward a focus on *being*, consciously resting in an alert awareness of the Spirit of Love. This state of mind, which requires no particular religious belief, frees us from our pre-occupations and agendas. It makes room for the Source of all life to flow through us—regardless of how we see ourselves in terms of religion or any other exterior identity—and provides the fertile ground for the active expression of love.

Pause

Here, once again, I invite you to create a pause in your busy day, a space to simply breathe, to relax, to settle your thoughts and emotions into a state of quiet awareness.

One of Ignatius's first followers, Francis Borgia, recommended these daily practices for cultivating humility:

> *As you get dressed in the morning, think of those who lack sufficient clothing.*
> *As you eat your meals, think of those who lack proper nourishment.*

As you go to bed at night, think of those who lack safety and shelter.

For Francis Borgia, these three moments of daily reflection helped cultivate Christ's humility and solidarity with the poor and the marginalized. Combined with gratitude—which recognizes that we cannot take credit for our many privileges—this practice forms the foundation for new attitudes about ourselves and our world.

Take a few minutes to reflect on Borgia's advice. How might you integrate it into your life? What reminders could you create (for example, an alarm on your phone) to call your attention to this expanded awareness of others?

As you leave this quiet pause, carry with you the intention to practice Borgia's daily ritual over the next week. Notice if you see any changes in the way you look at yourself and others. Make a note of anything new you learn.

14

Compassion

As I open myself to inner transformation,
I commit to the active compassion that brings exterior
transformation to communities and societies.

In this third stage of Ignatius's Spiritual Exercises, as he urges us to contemplate Jesus's pain and suffering, he once more asks us to use our imaginations. Don't do this in the abstract, he tells us, with the cushioning distance of time and space to protect you, but rather enter into Jesus's physical and emotional suffering. Stand at the foot of the cross where he died. Don't avoid the uncomfortable feelings that arise; instead, listen to them, sit with them, reflect on them. Remain present with Jesus. This, said Ignatius, is a spiritual experience that leads to inner regeneration. It allows us to not only suffer with Jesus but also see him in each hurting person. Jesus loved and embraced the marginalized, the condemned, the forgotten, the burdened, and the subjugated. Even as he went to his own death, he reached out with kindness and affirmation to those around him. He gave everything he had to the healing work of love.

As we look at Jesus's death as described in the Gospels, we see the reality of human suffering. There are no miracles, no last-minute rescues, no theological discourses about the meaning of death. Instead, we see a person who is thirsty, weak, exhausted, full of despair, and in terrible pain. With his death, Jesus challenges us to acknowledge the violence and pain that takes place every day in our world.

Jesus's expression of deep humility, Ignatius taught, asks us to set aside our self-preoccupation and consider the people around us. It demands that we give attentive concern to each individual, no longer treating other human beings as means to an end. We allow ourselves to feel the pain of those who suffer beneath our society's burden of intolerance and hatred. As we recognize the Divine Spirit in each person, we extend our love, respect, and active compassion.

Research on compassion indicates it includes an understanding that other people's suffering is real, an emotional sense of pain in response to that suffering, and a commitment to take action to address the suffering. For compassion to exist, according to this psychological definition, all three elements must be present. Compassion generates transformation, initially within our own hearts and minds, and then in the larger world around us.

Psychological research stresses that compassion is not the same thing as either pity or kindness. Pity is an expression of superiority and complacency. In effect, pity says, "It's too bad you're hurting—but boy, I'm glad *I'm* not in your situation." In contrast, compassion arises from a sense of shared humanity and solidarity. Pity is only an emotion, but compassion takes action. Meanwhile, a kind person may take care not to harm anyone in her immediate circle. She may even go out of her way to do nice things for others. In doing so, however, she never looks past the immediate boundaries of her world. Her "neighbors" are the people like her who live in her community and share her values. She would never steal food from an immigrant family; she would never intentionally harm a Black person or deny a Mexican child access to adequate medical care—but at the same time, she takes no action to dismantle the structures that create poverty, racism, and inequity. She's comfortable with the status quo.

Kindness and pity aren't enough. They don't compensate for unjust hiring practices that prevent women and Black people from holding better-paying leadership positions. They don't protect LGBTQIA adolescents who face bullying and social ostracism. They do nothing to help the 1.3 billion people who live in poverty around the world—or to provide clean water to communities whose water supply is polluted. They don't put an end to child labor, disability discrimination, inner-city food deserts, or police brutality. Kindness and pity don't transform our world.

Psychologists also define empathy as falling short of compassion. Neuroscientists have found that empathy activates pain-sensitive parts of the brain. Empathy brings tears to our eyes when we hear a news story about a school shooting or when we see the sad faces of hungry children in other countries. People with strong empathy reactions may pride themselves on their sensitivity—but at the same time, feeling others' suffering is unpleasant; it hurts, and so, just as we all tend to avoid painful situations, they may find themselves avoiding others' pain.

Empathy has other serious limitations. When people witness or imagine the pain of another person, the same neuro-networks light up on an MRI that would if the people were actually experiencing firsthand pain themselves—but studies have found that white people show far less neurological arousal when they witness a Black person's pain than when they are exposed to another white person's pain. Scientists hypothesize that from an evolutionary standpoint, empathy was useful only so far as it enabled people to cooperate with their own community. To feel empathy for someone outside the tribe would have been counterproductive to the safety of the tribe. Empathy, like kindness and pity, is not enough.

It turns out that the neural networks (as shown on magnetic resonance imagery) underlying empathy and compassion are very different. Whereas empathy often increases negative emotions, compassion activates neural networks connected with the emotional rewards of healthy relationships. Compassion is what gets parents out of a warm bed when their baby cries—and compassion is what spurs us to take action to protect and nurture the well-being of others.

As activist-author Glennon Doyle wrote, compassion is far more than a feeling; it is "a way of life . . . a habit that becomes a discipline." And, more than anything else, "compassion is a choice we make that love is more important than comfort or convenience."

Pause

Today, during these quiet moments, consider what the Charter for Compassion organization lists as twelve steps that lead to a more compassionate life.

Step 1: Learn about compassion. (Learn to recognize what it is and isn't in your emotions and behaviors.)

Step 2: Look at your own world. (Where do you see compassion already at work in the various communities to which you belong? Where do you see a lack of compassion that allows injustice to thrive?)

Step 3: Have compassion for yourself. (Guilt and shame over your own past behaviors can limit your expression of compassion in the present.)

Step 4: Practice empathy. (Make a conscious effort to tune into the feelings of others.)

Step 5: Practice mindfulness. (Set aside time each day for quiet reflection and awareness.)

Step 6: Take action. (Find opportunities every day to actively express love.)

Step 7: Acknowledge how little you know. (This ties compassion back to the humility we discussed in the last chapter. Compassion inspires you to let go of your certainties and be open to considering new points of view.)

Step 8: Pay attention to how you speak to and about others. (Notice when your words reflect an in-group/out-group orientation rather than solidarity with those in need.)

Step 9: Show concern for everybody. (Practice thinking of yourself as connected to the entire human race, as well as the entire planet—not just to the people you know and like or who are similar to you.)

Step 10: Widen your knowledge base. (Learn about other cultures and belief systems so that you can better understand others' perspectives.)

Step 11: Recognize pain where it exists. (Don't be like the passersby in Jesus's story who chose to ignore suffering.)

Step 12: Love your enemies. (Think about the people in your life you see as a threat to you—and then think of ways to be kind to them. Practice thinking of them as human beings who are a lot like you. Be willing to take action on their behalf.)

Reflect on how you might express each step in your own life. Pick two or three that speak to you particularly. Then, as you leave this small space of quiet awareness, carry those steps with you, at the back of your consciousness where you can return to them throughout the day whenever you have an opportunity. Consider the ways you can give compassion a greater space in your life. (To read more about the Charter of Compassion, go to https://charterforcompassion.org/charter.)

15

Surrender

*I release my need to be in control and to impress others,
so that I can enter into fuller, deeper expressions of love.*

"Take, O Lord, and receive my entire liberty, my memory, my understanding, and my whole will. All that I am and all that I possess, You have given me: I surrender it all to You for You to use as You will." This is the prayer of Ignatius of Loyola.

It's a tough act to follow. As a member of a religious order, I've surrendered my material possessions and many aspects of my freedom in ways my nonreligious friends often perceive as either nonsensical or unhealthy—but even as a religious person, I'm frankly terrified by the thought of giving up my abilities to think and to remember. I like my brain. And I also have to admit I like having a sense of control over my life.

Ignatius struggled with the same inner conflicts. Despite all the things he had already surrendered as he followed Jesus, he admitted to his followers that he still was constantly tempted by the desire to look good, to be in control, to have his achievements recognized. The ego-surrender that grows from humility did not come easily to him.

Before his conversion, he had thrown himself into dreams of being admired as a lover and a warrior; now he threw himself with equal passion into dreams of being recognized as a saint. When he gave up his fancy clothes, at first, he went around in rags, unwashed, his hair filthy and snarled—until he realized that by swinging to the opposite extreme of his former lifestyle, he was still calling attention to himself. As Ignatius became more practiced in self-awareness, he recognized this quality in himself, and he committed himself still more deeply to identifying with the humility and surrender of Jesus as he went to his death.

Jesus's embodiment of love offended the authorities of his day; they perceived his radical message of justice as a threat to their power. Those who enjoy power often maintain it by oppressing the vulnerable, and Jesus had made himself completely vulnerable. He did not do this easily, any more than any of us would in similar circumstances. He was not a masochist, finding warped pleasure in his own pain, and he had a healthy ego that resisted the thought of death. As he accepted that the consequence of his solidarity with the marginalized and downtrodden would likely mean the end of his life, he told his friends, "My soul is overwhelmed with sorrow"; clearly, he had the normal human reaction to the rejection, loneliness, and physical pain of what he was about to endure. Despite this, Jesus prayed to his Divine Parent, "Not what I will but what you will." The death Jesus accepted was violent, cruel, and ugly. As he accepted it, he demonstrated his absolute solidarity with all who are oppressed and hurting. He died to his own selfish concerns in order to give life to the cause of justice.

The concept of "dying to self" is often mentioned in religious circles, usually referring to our identification with Jesus's death on the cross. This vocabulary may make us squirm in discomfort. It seems to go against the grain of what we know today about emotional health. When the Spiritual Exercises tell us to imitate Jesus by choosing poverty rather than wealth and insults rather than honor, our natural reaction is to cringe and back away from Ignatius and his exercises. We think: *Now he's gone too far!* What healthy person longs for poverty, insults, and worthlessness?

In the Gospel of John, Jesus uses the metaphor of a seed to explain the self-surrender Ignatius was advocating, a seed that falls into the ground, where it rots, breaks, and disintegrates—so that a larger, more fruitful life can be released. When Jesus speaks of a "seed," it represents the outer shell of our identities, what we sometimes call our egos, the surface sense we have of who we are as individuals. Left to ourselves, we would never bury our shiny egos in the dirt, and we would do anything to protect them from being cracked, broken open so that our inner, secret selves are exposed. But as Jesus talks about seeds and soil, growth and fruit, he is telling us this: when we surrender the ego's need for prestige and control, new possibilities come into the world that never existed before. A far larger, more inclusive reality grows from the broken pieces of our egos.

And so, as we use our imaginations to connect with Jesus's experience on the cross, we see a radical form of self-surrender. Jesus gives himself away completely—not because he had an unhealthy need to suffer but as an act of absolute love. He dies so that something new can be born into the world.

Pause

Claim this small space of time as your own. Let yourself rest here for a few moments. For now nothing is required of you. Simply breathe: in, out; in, out.

When you feel quieted, both in your mind and in your body, ask yourself what comes to mind when you hear the word *surrender*. Do you think of defeat, humiliation, loss of power, even entrapment? Or do you think of love, humility, the willingness to change, the commitment to make a difference in the world? If you feel a mixture of reactions, can you sift through them, determining their sources within you or in your beliefs about the world?

It is not only Christianity that sees value in self-surrender. In the Hindu *Bhagavad Gita*, for example, Krishna—the Divine—says, "Abandon all varieties of purpose and simply surrender unto me alone. . . . Do not fear."

What is your response? Identify any emotions that arise in you. Imagine you can ask Krishna what he meant by this. What do you think his answer would be?

Spiritual teacher Eckhart Tolle says, "Surrender is to say 'yes' to life—and see how life suddenly starts working for you rather than against you." Does this give you a new understanding of what Jesus, Ignatius, and Krishna were talking about when they call us to self-surrender?

Carl Jung had this unusual definition of God: "the name by which I designate all things which cross my willful path violently and recklessly, all things which upset my subjective views, plans, and intentions and change the course of my life for better or worse." How does this relate to the concept of self-surrender we've been discussing in this chapter?

Mindfulness meditation is sometimes said to also be an act of surrender. By turning your awareness away from your regular preoccupations, you allow your smaller ego-self to drop away so that you can connect with your true, essential self, the part of you who lives in connection with the Divine. You surrender the small self with all its limitations so that you can enter your vast, eternal self.

What is your emotional response to all these ideas? Do you feel any clearer in your understanding of self-surrender? What questions remain?

As you go back to your ongoing life, carry these questions and reflections with you. Allow them to percolate in the back of your mind as you go about your day. Return to them tonight as you settle yourself for sleep. Consider specific ways that self-surrender might take shape in your life in healthy and life-giving ways.

Stage IV:

Hope, Joy, and Possibility

16

Responding
to the Resurrection

As I open myself to inner and outer transformation,
I also open myself to unexpected possibilities,
to startling new realities, and to hope that goes beyond
my greatest dreams.

In the fourth stage of the Spiritual Exercises, Ignatius directs us to look at the biblical narratives of Jesus's resurrection as the center point for a life of hope and active participation in the transformation of our world. During this stage, we once more experience the work of Divine love in every dimension of our lives, and we prepare to bring all we have learned on this spiritual journey back into our everyday routines.

As we reflect on the Gospel accounts of the resurrected Jesus, we see that his followers greeted him with fear and disbelief, as well as with joy and hope. In our lives, we too may be afraid when we are faced with the birth of something new and still unknown in our lives, something that seems impossible. We don't easily transition from sorrow into hope—and yet even the world of nature teaches us again and again that new life grows from death, like the seed Jesus described. The seeds of hope are found planted in sorrow.

The Gospels describe several incidents where the resurrected Jesus appears to his friends and followers. Each time, he meets them in the midst of their sorrow and fear— and then he leads them from despair and fear into dawning wonder and exuberant joy. This sense of new possibility does not ignore or minimize the world's suffering. Instead, it reaches out to embrace it with hope and love.

If you have difficulty believing that Jesus died and came back to life again, set those doubts aside for now. Ignatius was not developing any doctrine based on Jesus's resurrection; Ignatius never wrote theological treatises, but instead he expressed his solidarity with all of us when he shared his spiritual experiences with the world. What he did do was make explicit the implications of Jesus's life and death for how we live our lives. In this sense, the resurrection can be understood as a narrative about Divine power to revive the parts of our hearts and our world that have been wounded to the point of death.

Resurrection is the reality that creation is ongoing, constantly at work in our world, turning death into life again and again and again in ways we could never have expected. The resurrection of Jesus reveals a Divinity that is dynamic and active, not worn out or passive or static. It shows us the image of a God who is able to bring hope and life to even the deepest divisions and wounds.

In the Gospel accounts of the postresurrection Jesus, his friends do not instantly recognize him when they encounter him. When Mary Magdalene goes to his tomb and finds it empty, she cries out to the man she assumes is the gardener, not recognizing it is actually Jesus standing in front of her. Later, Jesus meets up with two of his friends as they are traveling along the road, but they don't recognize him either. Neither Mary nor these two friends of his expected to ever see Jesus again. They need time to see past their assumptions about the nature of death.

These stories suggest that resurrection can be hard to perceive at first. It's hard to see past our assumptions. Our initial reactions may not even be positive. Like Jesus's friends, we may be too mired in sadness to see any reason for joy. Even when we do recognize proof of new life where before we had seen only death, at first, our reaction may be fear. What does this new reality mean? What does it ask of us? How should we respond? Even when our hearts break open with the joy of this amazing and unexpected gift, like Jesus's friends, we will need time to let this new thing unfold within us. Our beliefs about the world may have been tipped upside down, and we need to be patient with ourselves as we let new realizations flow through us, changing us in unexpected ways.

Jesus gives Mary Magdalene, the first to see him after his resurrection, the job of telling others. Her grief and fear are transformed into a sense of purpose and meaning. She becomes a coworker with the Divine power that crackles out from the resurrection like electricity. The Jesus she loves is no longer limited to one person, one body; now she sees him everywhere. At the same time, her identity has changed as well. She is no longer bound by the limitations imposed on her by her society's expectations; now she has become the "Apostle to the Apostles." She has a vocation that gives her life new dignity and power.

Resurrection-possibility brings something similar to each of us: our expectations, our sense of what is feasible, and our confidence in spiritual forces may be too small, too confined. We may expect, for example, to find the Divine presence only in certain places and in certain ways; now, like Mary, we must let go of our familiar ways of understanding and relating to Divinity, and open ourselves to encountering the sacred in unexpected places. The resurrected Jesus challenges us, as he did Ignatius, to see God in everything and everyone—and in doing so, we, like Mary Magdalene and Ignatius of Loyola, find new vocations, new identities.

Ignatius challenges us to look for the new life that blossoms in our world as we participate in God's ongoing mission of justice, peace, and healing. To help us clear our clouded vision, Ignatius again reminds us to enter into the resurrection story with all the powers of our imagination.

Picture the resurrected Jesus. Reach out your hands and grab him by the arm. This Jewish, brown-skinned man has not been miraculously transformed into a mystical blonde-haired, blue-eyed white person who floats around in a disembodied realm of existence. His eyes and skin are still brown; he is still the unique person who was born in a barn, a member of a colonized people; and he is still concerned with the flesh-and-blood realities of our world.

Pause

Breathe. Consciously relax your muscles, one by one. Imagine your mind is a muscle you can also relax. Loosen any tightness you find there. Allow your mind to soften and open to new possibilities.

Now consider these four different responses to the resurrection that are described in the Gospels:

- Mary Magdalene, who overflows with longing and sorrow. She is seeking Jesus's dead body but, at first, finds only emptiness.
- Jesus's followers, who have gone into hiding after his death, afraid of the authorities who took Jesus's life.

- Thomas, one of Jesus's friends who earned the name "Doubting Thomas" because of his refusal to believe Jesus had come back to life.
- The two friends traveling away from the scene of Jesus's death, so filled with loneliness and grief that they cannot see the reality of Jesus's presence with them.

Which one of these responses do you most identify with right now?

If you are feeling empty and yearning, can you wait like Mary did at the tomb, until you experience something new that cannot be contained by your expectations?

If you are feeling afraid, your heart concealed where no one can see, can you allow Divinity to open the narrow space where you're hiding, surprising and startling you out of your fears?

If you are doubting the feasibility of new life at work in the world, can you hear the Divine invitation to reach out and touch a new reality?

If you are lonely, seeking connection, can you open your eyes to the Divine presence in the people around you?

Spend some time settling into the feeling of whichever story speaks most to you. Imagine yourself in that story, claiming it as your own. Then, as you return to the rest of your day, bring this story with you. Return to it before you fall asleep tonight. Allow it to open up fresh ideas in your mind and point you in new directions for action.

17

New Life

*I let go of all that is dead and unproductive in my beliefs,
in my personality, and in my interactions with others,
so that I can find a new identity filled with new purpose.*

The Gospels tell us that after the resurrection, Jesus comes to his friends as they are all gathered together, sad and fearful, and he startles them with his presence. They have been hiding out, afraid that they too might suffer Jesus's fate—and then suddenly, there he is with them. One of Jesus's friends, Thomas, who is not there at the time, refuses to believe the others when they tell him they have seen Jesus. He tells his friends he will have to see Jesus with his own eyes and touch him with his own hands before he will accept that something so impossible has taken place.

When Jesus shows up the next time, Thomas is there. Jesus turns to his friend and says, "Touch me. Put your hand on me. See my scars." With these words, Jesus invites us, as well as Thomas, into a new and transformed way of interacting with the tangible, visible world. All around us is the same magic that works in bean seeds and tulip bulbs. Ultimately, death does not triumph over life. Instead, death is a gateway into a far wider, deeper life.

After his resurrection, Jesus also has an encounter with his friend Peter. Peter, whose impetuous personality was a bit like Ignatius's, had fervently pledged to Jesus that he would follow him anywhere, even into death. Jesus responded to him, predicting that instead, Peter would deny him that very night, before the dawning of the next day. As Jesus was being tried by the authorities for the crimes of blasphemy and sedition (claiming to be Divine and challenging the authority of the Roman government), Peter followed at a distance. Several people recognized him and said to him, "Hey, aren't you a friend of that guy who's on trial?" But Peter denied his relationship with Jesus, just as Jesus predicted. When people persisted with their questions, Peter cursed and became even more emphatic in his denial. When he saw Jesus turn and look at him across the crowd, his heart must have cringed with shame. And so now, meeting Jesus after the resurrection, Peter needs to be reconciled with his friend. Peter's unfaithfulness and selfishness have created a break in their relationship—and after a breakfast Jesus prepares for his friends on the beach, Jesus and Peter have a private talk to mend their relationship.

Peter's story reminds us that there are many kinds of death besides the death of the body. One of the most painful forms is when our shiny ideals about our own selves fall dead at our feet. We believed ourselves to be talented, strong, courageous—and instead, we see we are broken, weak, and cowardly. Our old self-images wither up like caterpillars' worn-out chrysalises.

But, of course, we know what happens to those shriveled chrysalises. They break open so that something new, something amazing, something beautiful and unexpected can emerge. The butterfly metaphor for transformation has become so common that we may forget just how startling the whole business is: a fat, not particularly pretty, creepy-crawly worm hides itself away in its grave clothes, where it disintegrates, dies—and then, after time has gone by, emerges from its grave a totally new and unrecognizable creature, a being with bright wings and the power of flight.

This is what happened to Ignatius, just as it had happened to Peter. After their old images of themselves die, with time, something new comes from the dusty graves of their broken dreams. In Peter's beach conversation with Jesus, Jesus gives him a visionary vocation and calls him to a brand-new identity. The old hot-headed man is still there, but now he is no longer focused on himself. Jesus has charged him with the responsibility to feed "Jesus's sheep."

Jesus, with his fondness for metaphors, referred to himself many times throughout the Gospels as a shepherd, someone whose life is devoted to the care, guidance, and nurturing of creatures who are prone to getting lost and putting themselves in dangerous situations. The shepherd's job was a hard one, a twenty-four seven responsibility to ensure that the sheep were kept safe and that they had the sustenance and refreshment they needed to thrive. Now, as Jesus tells Peter to take over this job, he is in effect saying that Peter is to become like Jesus. Now Peter will also be a "good shepherd," devoting his life to the active work of promoting well-being in the lives around him. He will work to guide others on the safe paths that lead to life.

This story speaks to our own lives as well. It tells us that the "new life" of resurrection does not mean picking up and resuming our old dead lives. Instead, everything is changed. We find a sharper focus for our lives. We understand our identities in fresh ways.

When Jesus comes in his transformed, risen body to say goodbye to his friends, the Bible says he breathes on them. The Greek word translated as "breath" also means "spirit," and so Jesus is sending the Divine Spirit into his friends. This is a spiritual reality, but it is also the same breath that moves in and out of our bodies at this very minute (because there is no separation between spiritual and physical realities). The Source has breathed new life into us as well.

The Breath of Life is the undying energy that works for good in our world—and it breathes through each of us. Like Peter, we are each called to be Jesus, working for the good of those who need protection from the forces of destruction.

Pause

Relax into this quiet moment. Rest here for a few moments, focused on your breathing. Let everything else that has claimed your attention today drop away.

As each thing clamors for you to give it attention again—as it will—simply acknowledge it and return your focus to your breath.

Now think of yourself as you were when you were a baby. Picture the photographs you have seen of your infant self, and imagine what it must have felt like to be so small, so helpless, so unaware of the vast world beyond your experience.

In your mind's eye, watch as you grow, from baby to toddler, from toddler to older child, and from older child to adolescent. Note the changes in your body at each stage. Try to remember the changes you experienced emotionally and intellectually. What new experiences changed you? How did you think of yourself differently? Was it ever difficult for you to let go of a particular stage and move on into the next phase of your life? Were you afraid or sad—or did you greet the change and transformations of growing up with excitement, pride, and joy? How do you feel about these changes as you look back at them?

Become aware of the fact that change is continuing to happen within your body and within your mind. Open yourself to gratitude; thank yourself and the Divine for the life that continues to breathe through you, constantly remaking you.

As you look toward the future, how do you feel about the changes that inevitably lie ahead? Do you see them as little deaths that rob you of yourself—or can you see them as new lifeforms being born in you? How do you see your sense of your purpose in the world being shaped by these changes in your identity?

Spend some time reflecting on these thoughts. Be aware of your emotional responses. Do not force yourself to feel something you think you "should," simply note your feelings and then set them gently aside. Familiarize yourself with the challenge and promise of the changes that lie ahead of you.

18

Healing

I acknowledge the wounds in my own heart,
as well as in the world around me,
and I seek the power of Divine possibility
to restore and heal all that is damaged.

Ignatius bore emotional wounds. His mother died when he was young, and his father was harsh and distant. Ignatius tried to live up to the example of his older brothers, who were successful explorers and military men, but this got him in trouble on at least one occasion. Then, after his injury on the battlefield, he had to undergo several painful surgeries with no anesthesia. As he lay on his sickbed, he was in need of healing at many levels—physically, emotionally, spiritually. His healing process began in his first encounters with the life of Jesus, but it was not a fast or sudden process. Instead, over the months and years that followed, the work of Divine healing would spread slowly through his body, his emotions, his behaviors, and his interactions. In the resurrected Jesus, Ignatius found a model for the healing power he needed to bring him peace, resolution, and hope.

The Gospels make clear that physical reality—including human flesh, blood, and bone—is important to Jesus. His touch heals bodies, and his own body is real and present, not "spiritual" in the sense that it has no physical shape: he eats and sleeps, breathes and cries. He spits, his feet get dirty, and his stomach gets empty. His body is like yours and mine, and like our bodies, his flesh contains Divinity. After the resurrection, the Gospels describe his body as transformed, possessing new abilities (like walking through walls and appearing and disappearing), but it is still real and solid. The risen Jesus is not a ghost, drifting around in wisps of ectoplasm; he can be seen and touched. He can cook his friends a meal on the beach, and then join them in eating it.

Christianity has sometimes glossed over this. Many of us find it easier to believe in the abstract and spiritual Jesus, the Jesus who saves from sin and takes us all to heaven, rather than the Jesus who continues to be in the here and now of our reality, demanding that we pay attention to his presence. The resurrection is such a tall claim, one that counteracts everything we know about reality that it's far easier to either dismiss it as legend, with no implications for how we live out our lives, or turn it into a purely spiritual event. We forget the scarred hands, the wounded belly, the breakfast on the beach, and we turn Jesus into a "heavenly Friend," a shining, celestial person whose only concern is with "spiritual matters." Ignatius, however, saw in the resurrection the human Jesus, the flesh-and-blood man, and Ignatius understood the resurrection to mean that we too are called to bring healing and resurrection wherever we see Jesus's suffering and death in the world around us.

We all bear wounds. We have been wounded by misunderstandings and disappointment, wounded by fear and rejection, wounded by the systemic violence of our world. Ignatius believed his Spiritual Exercises were the road map to a journey of healing, restoring life and well-being to both our inner beings and the exterior world around us. We participate in this healing actively with our bodies and our minds and our hearts. Divine resurrection brings life and health back to damaged muscles and nerves, as well as to the neural networks of our brains. It corrects our misguided frames of reference and mends our imperfect visions of the world. It builds bridges of reconciliation between people separated by prejudice and hatred.

Ignatius came to understand that in most cases, healing is simply the consequence of following in the footsteps of the resurrected Jesus. We do not need to engage in magical healing ceremonies or ask for miracles; healing simply unfolds, slowly and naturally, sometimes almost imperceptibly. As we allow our inner lives to be transformed, those changes express themselves in the external world with the ever-spreading work of reconciliation.

In the early days of his conversion, however, Ignatius thought it was up to him to somehow manufacture experiences of healing and reconciliation. He engaged in brutally honest and lengthy confessions, with an obsessive need to remember *every single sin* he had ever committed. He punished his body with extreme penances, nearly starving himself to death. He planned to go on a pilgrimage to the Holy Land, hoping this would prove he has entered into a new and holier phase of his life. But none of these strategies accomplished what he hoped they would. Finally, he accepted that the way to inner and outer reconciliation would first lead him deep within himself.

At this point, Ignatius was ready to be reconciled with his past, with his failures and shame. He also entered into a new ministry of reconciliation and healing in response to the brokenness he saw in his world. He no longer sought to find healing in stupendous feats of ascetic holiness; now he worked to answer the calls for justice and reconciliation he perceived in the tangible, societal world. He and his followers built schools and hospitals. They created safe homes for women who had been forced into prostitution. A quote that's often attributed to Ignatius is: "If our church is not marked by caring for the poor, the oppressed, the hungry, we are guilty of heresy." Ignatius understood that faith is a practical thing, an active thing, not just a spiritual feeling we tuck away in our hearts.

In the Middle Ages, the Latin root word for today's *reconciliation* meant "to restore to union and friendship after estrangement or variance." This is the work of healing that both Ignatius and Jesus call us to practice. It allows new realities to take shape, and it empowers us with the strength and energy to move toward new horizons of justice and freedom for all people.

The gifts of new life and healing that the resurrected Jesus brought to his friends did not stop with them. Instead, they were like the yeast Jesus used as a metaphor for what he called the reign of heaven, something invisible but alive that gives the entire mass new shape, new energy, new possibility.

Pause

Take a moment now to let yourself simply rest, as though you were a baby held in the arms of someone who loves you infinitely. Let a sense of love and total security flow through you with each inhalation of your breath.

Now think back to Ignatius's Examen, which we outlined in the introduction. The five steps described there can also be seen as a formula for personal growth. Here is a different version of the Examen, which you can apply to the restorative work of healing.

1. Seek enlightenment.
In other words, enlarge your perspective. Recognize the false assumptions that have limited your life spiritually, socially, and emotionally.

2. Express gratitude.

Psychologists recommend we break negative mental cycles by focusing on positive things. This doesn't instantly erase interior hurt or exterior suffering, but it creates a space where you can begin to glimpse new possibilities.

3. Recognize your emotions.

Identify any hurts that have accumulated in your mind and heart. Look at their causes, the circumstances that wounded you. Be curious about each situation. See if you can identify other ways to interpret or understand the situation.

4. Be ready to take positive action.

No matter how much you hurt, pain does not justify retaliation. Breaking the cycle of negative action and reaction is a step toward healing. As you let go of the past, your vision will be cleared to see new possibilities for the future.

5. Anticipate tomorrow.

Ignatius advises that you daily make a resolution to be the best possible version of yourself. Don't settle for mediocrity or lukewarm love. Always strive to be *more*, allowing the Divine to use you in new and radical ways.

19

The Divine Dream

*As I come to understand the Divine Dream
for the health and healing of the world,
I will participate in the Spirit that is constantly at work
to make that dream a reality.*

Throughout *The Spiritual Exercises*, Ignatius, like Jesus in the Gospels, wrote often of "the kingdom of God" or the "realm of heaven." In today's language, we might better describe this as the Divine Dream for our world. Both Ignatius and Jesus were talking about God's vision of the world as it could be, if nothing was broken, if no arrow had missed its mark, if every aspect of human society was aligned with love.

Most of us are familiar with Martin Luther King Jr.'s famous declaration "I have a dream," a dream in which he envisioned a reality that would grow out of the limitation and racism of the world as he knew it in the 1960s, a dream of a healthier way of life that would spread and deepen into a more just, more equitable society where all are equal, all are protected, and all are honored and valued. Despite racism's ongoing reality, King's dream has never died. It is still unfolding. It continues to inspire us and push us to become better versions of ourselves.

Jesus also had a dream for the present that would need to be lived into the future. In the Gospel of John, after the resurrection, Jesus expressed his dream in a prayer:

> I have a dream that all my followers will experience my joy. I have a dream that my followers will carry the truth into the world. I have a dream that they will all be one, just as I am one with the Divine; that they too will be One with Divinity—me in them, and God in me—so that all their divisions are healed and they come together in complete unity. I have a dream that love will shine through them into the world, so that all the world comes to understand the true meaning of Divinity.

Because Jesus spoke of the "realm of heaven," his followers have often mistaken his meaning. They have assumed he was talking about the "spiritual world," a reality we will not experience until after we die, and then only if we "believe" in Jesus. This form of faith excuses us from doing the work of justice: feeding the hungry, visiting people in prison, healing the broken, and working to create a society where everyone has access to educational and professional opportunities, as well as adequate medical care. If heaven only exists in some vague and faraway spiritual realm, and our religious beliefs are the only standard required for admittance, then Christ's followers will direct their energy to proselytizing for Christianity. Jesus, however, said the realm of heaven is among us or "nearby." It is here and now, on the Earth, not an afterlife reward waiting only for those who claim to believe in Jesus. Genuine "belief in Jesus" always results in taking action to help and support humans in need. It creates a mindset where we experience kinship with all creation.

Martin Luther King Jr. referred to the realm of heaven as something very present, the "Beloved Community," his global vision for a world where all people share and protect the Earth's wealth. In King's Beloved Community, poverty, hunger, and homelessness are no longer tolerated. Racism and all forms of discrimination, bigotry, and prejudice are erased, and the all-inclusive spirit of sisterhood and brotherhood blossoms everywhere.

The Christian scriptures speak of the *pleroma*, a state of fullness and completion that is the embodiment of Divinity in the physical world, the full expression of the Divine Dream. This is a reality that is both *now* and *not yet*. It exists in the mind of God, but we do not yet see its full expression in our world.

This interconnected and complete unity is also sometimes called the Body of Christ, which we mentioned in chapter 10. "Just as a body is one whole made up of many different parts," wrote Paul, one of Jesus's first-century followers, "and all the different parts comprise the one body, so it is with [Jesus]." Paul went on to say:

> No matter our heritage—Jew or Greek, insider or outsider—no matter our status—oppressed or free—we were all given the one Spirit to drink. Here's what I mean: the body is not made of one large part but of many different parts. Would it seem right for the foot to cry, "I am not a hand, so I couldn't be part of this body"? Even if it did, it wouldn't be any less joined to the body. And what about an ear? If an

ear started to whine, "I am not an eye; I shouldn't be attached to this body," in all its pouting, it is still part of the body. Imagine the entire body as an eye. How would a giant eye be able to hear? And if the entire body were an ear, how would an ear be able to smell? . . . So now, many members function within the one body. The eye cannot wail at the hand, "I have no need for you," nor could the head bellow at the feet, "I won't go one more step with you." It's actually the opposite. The members who seem to have the weaker functions are necessary to keep the body moving. . . . God designed the body in such a way that greater significance is given to the seemingly insignificant part. That way there should be no division in the body; instead, all the parts mutually depend on and care for one another. If one part is suffering, then all the members suffer alongside it. If one member is honored, then all the members celebrate alongside it. You are the body of [Jesus]: each and every one of you is a vital member.

Paul was using the extended metaphor of the body to explain the Divine Dream.

One translation of the Greek-based word *pleroma* has to do with being in a boat. We can also see this boat as a metaphor for God's Dream, a reality where all are included and carried to a safe destination. No one is left out to drown.

The Western world's social model has failed to recognize this reality. Instead, we often act as though different groups of people have their own boats. We worry about what will keep our own "boat" afloat, and we fail to recognize the needs of people we believe are sailing in separate ships. We may feel empathy when we see images on the news of people who are figuratively drowning (and sometimes literally, in the case of refugees seeking safety on the other side of the sea)—but we always have the option to turn off the news. We return our gaze to the sights we can see from the restricted perspective of our own little watercrafts, unaware that in reality, we are all sailing in the same ship.

God's Dream encompasses the entire cosmos, working in all things to bring Divine love into physical reality. Each aspect of our world interacts with everything else. In this living web of relationship, you can't pull on one strand without shaking all the other threads in the web. Throughout the Gospels, Jesus describes this "realm" and invites us to join him there.

And our hearts' deepest desires also express the same dream Jesus had. In the Spiritual Exercises, Ignatius calls us to perceive this vision of life—a life of justice, inclusion, and love—and then respond with both our hearts and our bodies. In doing so, we participate with the Source of all life, building the Divine Dream in the tangible and visible world. As theologian Howard Thurman wrote, "A dream is the bearer of a new possibility, the enlarged horizon, the great hope."

Pause

Find a relaxed position, and then focus on your breathing. Simply be aware of it, without trying to slow your breathing or speed it up. Notice how the air feels as it enters your nostrils. Be aware of the sensation the air makes as it moves down your throat and into your lungs. Feel the exhale as the air leaves your body. Do this until you feel quiet and settled.

Now imagine the story in the Gospel where the risen Jesus comes to his friends and breathes on them. Picture yourself among his friends. Feel the warmth of his breath on your face. Another story, this one from the Hebrew scriptures, says God gave life to human beings by breathing into them. With these stories in mind, return your attention to your own breath. Allow yourself to sense that the Divine is breathing through you. Your breath is God's breath.

Now expand your awareness to other people and animals in your area (other members of your household, people walking by on the sidewalk, your companion animals, birds and squirrels in the trees). Sense the constant in-and-out of all these beings' breaths. Their breath is God's breath.

Expand your awareness even further. Open your mind and heart to plants and trees and even microscopic organisms. They too have their own form of breath. Reflect on God's breath in all these creatures.

Finally, widen your perception to include the entire Earth. Imagine you can hear the constant breath that flows through all life. This too is the Divine breath.

Rest here for a moment, feeling your connection to the Divine and to all life. When you are ready, return to your ordinary life, but continue to be aware of the sacred connections that interweave your life with all other lives. Reflect on how the shared breath of Divinity relates to the Divine Dream.

20

The Empowerment of Possibility

I will open my eyes to the possibilities
hidden in our world's problems,
so that I can be empowered
to become something greater,
to try more, and to do better.

Ignatius believed Divine love is always entering our world. In a mystical vision, he saw this love flowing out from God and returning to God, an ongoing cycle as constant as our breath. When we commit ourselves to active involvement with this life-giving respiration, we allow the Divine Dream to manifest itself more and more in the world around us.

Ultimately, the story of the resurrection is a call to *imagine*—to see past the limitations of our world to new vistas, to broaden our perspectives, to open our hearts and minds to the fullness of the Divine Dream. Divine imagination has no limits, and in the Spiritual Exercises, Ignatius challenges us to extend our own capacity for possibility. With the eyes of our imagination (as we discussed in chapter 7), we see beyond current conditions, past the broken reality we have taken for granted, to the potential hidden like seeds in the world's soil. "The Possible's slow fuse," wrote poet Emily Dickinson, "is lit by the Imagination." The seeds of possibility may grow slowly—but they are alive and real and present.

The empowerment of possibility reveals a world that is better, greater, more. In *The Spiritual Exercises*, Ignatius uses those three words—*better, greater, more*—again and again. He never says we should stop being "bad" and become "good," as though goodness was a particular endpoint we can reach and then rest on our laurels. Instead, he asks us to move from "good" to "better." The Spiritual Exercises are a map to a spirituality that's not content with a passive, static, mediocre way of life. Instead, they spur us to love more, reach out further, envision greater justice, and build stronger bridges to freedom and opportunities for everyone.

As a member of the Society of Jesus, I have learned to use the Latin word *magis* (which means "more, greater") to express Ignatius's invitation to go higher and farther. The term *magis* also refers to "the greater good"—the pleroma, the Divine abundance that flows into the world, filling in the gaps, completing the places that are lacking, incarnating Divinity everywhere. This is what Ignatius calls us to seek: the unlimited possibility of God.

Magis summons us to actively participate in its vision, expanding our imaginations and energizing our efforts, leading us toward a world where all people and communities experience the fullness of life. The "greater good" of *magis* applies to everyone. As Divine love is incarnated in us and through us, no one is excluded or pushed to the margins. The well-being of each individual is necessary to the health and happiness of us all.

As we work to constantly make our world better, we learn the meaning of hope. We cannot know what the future holds, but, as activist Gustavo Gutiérrez said, we face the future with openness, "in an attitude of spiritual childhood," accepting the gift of the possibilities that lie ahead. Hope holds us steady, even when the current reality may seem hopeless. It keeps our vision focused beyond the limitations of the present so that we can resist things as they are and work to build something better. Rather than insisting on a particular outcome, hope is open to the surprise and mystery of the possible. Hope orients our lives, allowing us to see the Divine Dream shining through the world as it is, empowering us to keep working to bring the dream of justice out into the light of day, where everyone can share and participate in it.

Hope is not naive, idealistic, or unrealistic. It clearly recognizes real-life problems and challenges, but at the same time, it sees the possibilities that lie hidden in current realities. Theologian Jürgen Moltmann wrote:

> Hope alone is to be called "realistic," because it alone takes seriously the possibilities with which all reality is fraught. It does not take things as they happen to stand or to lie, but as progressing, moving things with possibilities of change.

Ignatius said that consolation is a "gentle increase of faith, hope, and love." Consolation and hope work together. They pull us toward the future. According to Ignatius, the "increase of hope . . . calls and attracts heavenly things" (the things that are characteristic of the Divine Dream). Hope also, he said, brings health and healing to the soul, "quieting it and giving it peace."

The Spiritual Exercises promise us that each of us has the ability to change the world, one small action at a time. As stewards of Divine love, sharing it with those around us in concrete and practical ways, we discover that love is powerful and creative. As we open ourselves wider and wider to contain its abundance, we are transformed within—and empowered to discover and build new possibilities in the world around us.

Pause

Carol Dweck, the author of *Mindset: The New Psychology of Success*, defines a fixed mindset versus a growth mindset as two different ways we can think about our abilities, mistakes, and hopes for the future. People with a fixed mindset think failure means they have reached the end of the road; they see nowhere else to go in that direction, and so they turn away in discouragement. People with a growth mindset, however, think failure is an opportunity to grow; they see possibility instead of a dead end.

Dweck says we can train ourselves to have a growth mindset by devoting at least five minutes a day to learning something new. This can be anything—for example, a foreign language, a craft, a musical instrument, or historical or scientific information. By doing this, she says, we build our ability to perceive and participate in possibilities instead of dead ends.

In today's quiet pause, think of something you would like to learn. Make a plan that breaks this down into short, doable, daily steps—and then commit yourself to that plan.

Rest for a moment before you return to your day—and then, as you put this book aside, take with you this resolution: to first notice Divine possibilities, and then to work to bring them into embodiment.

Stage V:

The Meaning of Divine Love

21

A Love Story

I open myself to Divine love,
so that my entire life becomes a love story.

Ignatius began his Exercises with the affirmation that the unconditional love of God is the foundation of our spiritual journeys. Now he ends the Exercises with an invitation to go even deeper into Divine love. In doing this, he builds on the earlier stages of the Exercises, bringing them together into a united narrative of love.

He refers to this part of his Exercises as a "contemplation," but it is an active experience of reciprocal self-giving rather than an intellectual exercise. We are intimately connected to the Source of all life, just as we are intimately connected to other human beings and to the Earth, and it is these deep connections that sustain us and give us life. They are the ordinary reality we experience each day, a part of our ongoing growth, our ever-deepening capacity to participate in life and love. This love, the fiber of the cosmos, does not need to be earned in order to access it. It is already present with us; our goal now is to consciously receive it and give it—to make our entire lives a love story.

A story puts random events together and makes sense of them. It perceives a pattern in the midst of chaotic circumstances. It creates a narrative that gives meaning to life. The story that Ignatius invites each of us to make our own follows the example of Jesus, countering hatred with love. It refuses to let violence and destruction have the last word at the end of the story—and it also refuses to let negative forces shape the meaning of our past.

Love is not limited by our linear concept of time. It shines its light on the present moment, on the road ahead, and also on the road behind us, sweeping up even the most painful and ugliest elements of the past into its creative embrace. With the eyes of love, we learn to see our past differently. We discover our lives have, all along, right from the beginning, been love stories.

Ignatius wrote more about love in his *Constitutions* (the outline for the structure of the Jesuits as a religious order). There, he described what he called *discreta caritas*—the discernment of love. Discernment (which we initially discussed in chapter 9) allows us to filter out any selfishness or other "disordered" emotion (see chapter 4) so that our love is pure, in the sense that it is cleansed from anything that would dilute it or diminish its power.

The *Constitutions* stress the need for "wise love," a love that directs itself outward with gentleness and respect. This love is adaptable, not intolerant, and flexible rather than rigid in its expectations and demands. It creates balance within our hearts and minds, and also in the way we interact with the world. It teaches us to build on hope and possibility with patience and realistic expectations. It shows us how to merge our inner intimacy with the Divine with the active love we express to our "neighbors" (see chapter 14), creating a synergy of empowered love.

This wise love avoids the pitfalls of too much and too little. Staying between the extremes, it practices moderation, the "Middle Way" we described in the introduction. At the same time, it does not contradict the Ignatian call to *magis*—to constantly seek more love, committing to love that works harder and does more (chapter 20). The discernment Ignatius describes is not meant to limit our devotion to learning, expansion, and self-improvement.

In *The Spiritual Exercises*, Ignatius wrote that he would, in effect, rather be considered emotionally unstable or lacking in intelligence because of his commitment to Jesus than be thought wise and sensible because of his conformity to his society's expectations. The practice of discernment did not hold back his love or make it more credible in the world's eyes. Instead, *discrete caritas* and *magis* worked together to dig an efficient channel for the stream of love rushing through him. Ignatius's entire life became a connecting conduit between himself, God, and others.

Love allows us to be increasingly less dependent on rules and restrictions to shape our spiritual lives. Instead, the love the Spirit "engraves" on our hearts, said Ignatius, becomes the only rule, the only restriction. Divine love allows us to see clearly where our desires and fears are warping our love; it reveals the possibilities disguised by the world's impossibilities while also recognizing realistic capabilities and capacities. It takes into account the limitations of people and circumstances, times and places, empowering us to participate in love's eternal creation. We are part of the infinitely flexible Divine response that "works together all things for good."

This level of love requires spiritual and emotional maturity. We cannot expect ourselves to reach it quickly or easily, and if we have not yet reached this level, we need not feel guilt or frustration. Instead, we simply commit to building on our potential for deeper love. We acknowledge that mature love is at the center of the Divine Dream unfolding within us and all around us, and in trust, we surrender all that is broken or off-target within us to the never-ending work of love.

Most stories have a plot, a line of action that runs through them, and Ignatius teaches us over and over that love must be put into action. Our sacred love story may begin with inner "movements"—emotions that inspire and encourage us—but strong emotions are not enough. This love story's action continually spreads outward, sweeping up all creation into its plotline.

Pause

Take a few moments to rest in a quiet pause, either sitting or lying down. Breathe in and out, riding the waves of your breath until you feel you have reached a steady level of moment-to-moment awareness.

Now picture someone who loves you—or loved you—unconditionally. (If you can't bring to mind such a person, focus as specifically as you can on an imagined person. It might be someone you encountered in a book, from a story told to you, from history, or from the realm of justice.) Feel how that love wraps around you, regardless of your failures or limitations. Imagine yourself floating in a sea of love that has no end or beginning. If feelings of unworthiness arise, set them aside as irrelevant. You do not have to overcome those feelings because unconditional love does not need to be earned.

Take those feelings and bring them inside you now so that unconditional love flows both into you and from you. As you wrap others in love, you also wrap yourself in total acceptance. Imagine that you hear all reality—the Earth, the trees and other plants, the sea and stars, the animals and the entire human community—whispering: *Be happy. Be safe. Be protected. Be free from inner and outer oppression. Be healthy and whole.* Join the prayer, repeating these same words, claiming them for yourself, even as you send them out to the cosmos. Remember, you cannot love others unless you love yourself, and you cannot love yourself if you do not love others.

Continue to repeat the words of this prayer, wrapping them around your own heart, even as you use them to embrace other individuals and circumstances in your life. Start with the people who are closest to you, both emotionally and physically, and then widen this sea of intentional and unconditional love until it stretches as far as your imagination can take you, including marginalized groups of people, as well as politicians and government leaders, and situations on the other side of the planet, as well as those that are in your own local community. Intentionally choose to send love to people you find difficult to like, for whatever reason.

Then shift your focus to people who are exploited; to anyone who is at the mercy of enemies who oppress them; to people who are imprisoned, justly or unjustly; to anyone who is in the hospital, sick or dying; to those who live surrounded by the chaos and suffering of war; to children and adults living in poverty, without opportunities for healthy nutrition, quality education, professional opportunities, or adequate medical care; and to all people of color, women, nongender-normative individuals, and anyone else who suffers because of prejudice and discrimination.

If you find your mind wandering or your emotions rebelling, return your focus to your breath until you are once more relaxed and at peace.

Mindfulness expert Jack Kornfield says that the daily practice of meditations like this is similar to practicing piano scales: the more faithful you are to a daily practice, the more adept and proficient you will be overall as you play your love story to yourself and to the world.

When you feel ready to leave this moment, carry your prayer with you and repeat it in any open spaces in your day or as you are falling asleep tonight: *Be happy. Be safe. Be protected. Be free from inner and outer oppression. Be healthy and whole.* Allow this prayer to shape your thoughts, your attitudes toward yourself and others, and your outlook on the world around you. Be open to expressing this prayer in action whenever opportunities reveal themselves.

22

The Beloved World

I affirm that love is woven through the cosmos,
and I seek to open myself to that love,
extending active and unconditional love even as I receive it.

As we finish this final stage of the Spiritual Exercises, we hear the call to enter into a new relationship with the world around us. We do this not out of duty or guilt but out of love. We see with new eyes. We look at one another and recognize the image of God. The goodness and beauty we find in each other draw us ever deeper into Divine goodness and beauty, summoning us to mutual care for one another and for our world.

Divine love, taught Ignatius, makes every aspect of life sacred. It unifies all things—thought and action, spiritual and physical—as well as all people. Built on this perspective, the Spiritual Exercises challenge us to experience life in a radically new way, encountering the Divine in everything we see and touch, everything we do and say, everything we think and feel, and in every person we encounter.

"God works and labors for me in all things created on the face of the earth," said Ignatius. Some people have misinterpreted the teachings of the Hebrew and Christian scriptures to justify exploiting nature and its resources, but that is not what Ignatius is saying here. Instead, his words imply the Source of life is also like a woman in labor who never ceases to birth something new into the world. This process is going on all around us, all the time. The Divine is being born not only in you and me but in every human being, in every living thing, and in every circumstance and situation. Ignatius wrote:

> God dwells in creatures: in the elements, giving them being; in plants, giving them life; in animals, giving them sensation; in humans, giving them understanding; and finally in me, giving me being,

animating me, giving me sensation, and making me to understand; likewise making a temple of me, being created in the image and likeness of Divine Majesty.

Each and every atom of the universe is striving to burst into Divinity.

God, said Ignatius, is the Source of all reality, and God at the same time emerges from all reality, "as rays descend from the sun" and "waters from a fountain." His words here echo the vision he had (see chapter 20), where he saw all things coming from Divinity while also returning to Divinity.

The Divine Presence is dynamic and continuous; it never stops moving forward, bringing us ever nearer to the Divine Dream. Following Ignatius's example, we learn to perceive the Divine not only in the people and things that bring us joy but also in our struggles and challenges, both big and small. We look back at the past, and there we see God's Dream unfolding in history, both our own and the larger histories of our communities and our world. We perceive history itself as a sacred expression of the Divine, and we look for that active and loving presence in the unfolding of new possibilities in our present world, as well as the world we are building for the future.

Every element of reality expresses Divine love, and so the world in its entirety also becomes our beloved. As we naturally give to the people we love, caring for them and working to ensure their well-being, that sense of tenderness and responsibility extends farther and farther. Because we love people of color, we seek to build a world that is free of racism. Because we love people who belong to the LGBTQIA community, we work to ensure that our society accepts them and extends to them the rights to self-expression, committed love, and family life. Because we love children and older people, we do all we can to create a world where each individual is loved, honored, and cared for. Because we love every aspect of the Earth, the source of our physical life, we dedicate ourselves to healing and protecting her. We stand in awe before the Divine Presence in each face and facet of our world. We see each person's beauty, strength, gifts, and power. As we allow love to flow into us, we open our hearts to return that love, entering into a spirit of giving that excludes no one.

Ignatius believed that in our conversations with the Divine, we should feel free to ask for the "grace" we need.

By this, he meant we confidently request from God, like a secure and well-loved child asking for food, all that we most deeply long for. Grace, said Ignatius, is the unearned gift of Divine love. We ask for grace to grow in loving the way God loves so that our entire being is swept up in love, uniting us with all people.

As we give and receive, joined in the constant, reciprocal respiration of love, we grow into a deeper understanding of what it means to be a part of the breathing network of life. And finally, since God is present in all things, when we ask for grace, ultimately, we are asking for God.

Pause

During this pause, try something different. Instead of finding a quiet place to sit, go for a walk, if you are physically able (and if you aren't, go for a walk in your imagination). As you walk, at first focus on your breath, as you have done before, but this time, allow your attention to shift to each thing you encounter. Whatever you see—another person, cars, buildings, trees, birds, the sun, the sky, blades of grass, *everything*—say to yourself,

Here, now—simply THIS, and give your attention to that person or thing for as long as you can. Recognize the presence of the Divine.

Continue to do this as you walk. As you notice each thing, greet it, however you want. Say hello. Affirm that here, now, in *this*, the Divine is present. Then, as you walk on, leaving it behind, wish it well and bid it goodbye (perhaps using the old form of *goodbye*: "God be with you").

When you reach a place where it makes sense for you to be still for a few moments (perhaps a park bench, the steps of a building, or a scenic spot on a bridge), stop your walk and simply look. Be aware of tiny details: a falling leaf, a colorful barrette in a child's hair, the gleam of light on a pigeon's feathers. After a few moments, shift your attention to your ears: notice each sound, loud and soft. Then be aware of your skin: *What does the air feel like against your face? How does the sun feel on your head? What surfaces do you touch with your fingers? What does the earth feel like beneath your feet? How do your clothes feel against your skin?* Finally, taste and smell the air. Identify as many scents and flavors as you can.

Now close your eyes and breathe in, slowly and deeply. Feel through your breath your connection to the sky, to the cosmos, to the Earth. Open your heart in love and express your gratitude. Say "thank you" for the nourishment and beauty the Earth gives. Imagine love flowing out from you around the entire planet, with all its different peoples and varying crises, and out into space. Embrace the stars—and feel yourself embraced in return. Allow each breath you inhale to bring love into you, and with each exhale, send your love out into the world.

When you feel ready to move on, do so, returning to your ordinary life. As you go through the rest of your day, be aware of the presence of love in each person and thing you see—and consciously send out love in return.

23

Generous Action

Knowing the Divine loves me unconditionally,
I respond to the world's needs with love and action.

As we more and more surrender our attachment to things, as well as to our own control (see chapter 13), we enter a growing largeness of spirit, an openhearted generosity that makes room for Divine love to flow through us, reaching past all human barriers so that we give of ourselves across the borders of religion, race, gender, education, and class. This leads us to the "more" that Ignatius described, the concept Jesuits think of as *magis* (see chapter 20). This "more" is a longing, a heart's desire, an ever-present yearning for a better world, a world more aligned with the Divine Dream. It calls us to expand our inner and outer lives more than we ever thought we could, not only for ourselves but also on behalf of the larger reality in which we live.

We discover we don't have a spiritual identity that's separate from the rest of our lives. Instead, the life of the Spirit is lived in everything we do. As we go to work, change diapers, sit at a computer, wash the dishes, interact with customers, play with children, or participate in meetings, we engage in spiritual work. When we do the laundry, mow the lawn, prepare a meal, or mop the floor, we participate in the Spirit's flow. Our creativity—no matter what form it takes—is an expression of Divine love, and each of our interactions with the people in our lives is also an opportunity to express love. We realize all the aspects of our lives are potential points of connection to a deeper reality.

The *magis* can also take the form of longing and yearning—a heart's desire for what is still beyond us, for all that is still hidden within the Divine Dream. It is the challenge to become "ever more" for God as we build a world of ever-greater justice and love. This is the challenge woven into the Spiritual Exercises.

As we integrate the stages of the Spiritual Exercises, we begin to enter into each day with a sense of reverence, honoring the Living Spirit that is everywhere we turn. We hear the call to treat others with kindness and respect. Recognizing their dignity and worth, we take action on behalf of those who suffer from injustice, and we recognize our responsibility to care for the planet that gives us life. We let the Spirit of Love flow through us into the world. We seek to let our lives make a difference, as they embody the Divine Dream. We realize that within the interwoven community of life, the "greater good" is always expressed through our interdependent solidarity with one another. A live-and-let-live attitude has no room here, for our existence is woven together in a single fabric.

This outlook leads to what Ignatius called "magnanimity." We usually define this word as a synonym for "generosity," but we find a deeper meaning when we look at the English word's Latin roots: *magna* ("great") + *anima* ("soul"). Literally, then, the word means "great soul." A person who possesses magnanimity in this sense sees past all her assumptions about reality's limitations and develops a wider outlook. She thinks big, recognizing that the Divine wants her to express the fullness of her potential, even as she works to empower others to develop their full potential as well. As she envisions new possibilities, she is empowered by hope; gratitude and generosity guide her actions.

Ignatius believed that as we see God everywhere, in everything and everyone, our natural response will be "love and service." Thought, emotion, and action merge. Aware we are unified with the rest of the world, essential to its well-being, we live our lives in a radically new way, responding to the challenge and call of love wherever we hear it. (And we hear it everywhere!)

The Divine Dream is constantly ready to be born; it waits patiently at every opening, ready to emerge, blossom, and grow. It enters the world through relationships with the people we love—and it bursts out, taking us by surprise, when we reach out to those who are separated from us by beliefs, behaviors, or appearance. It flows into the world through protest marches, petitions to Congress, and boycotts—and through the ordinary, daily practices of kindness and inclusion. Fear and distrust make our world small and ugly, but the magnanimity of the Divine Dream widens, deepens, and brings beauty wherever it is expressed.

In the *Constitutions of the Society of Jesus*, Ignatius defined this generosity of soul we are called to experience and express, saying that magnanimity allows us to:

bear the weaknesses of many, initiate great undertakings in the service of God our Lord, and persevere in them with the needed constancy, neither losing courage in the face of the contradictions, even from persons of high rank and power, nor allowing [ourselves] to be deflected by their entreaties or threats from what reason and the Divine service require. [We] should be superior to all eventualities, not letting [ourselves] be exalted by success or cast down by adversity.

"Stop settling for small, for stunted, for shrunken," Ignatius says to us in the Spiritual Exercises. "Claim the infinite space of Divine love as your own. Secure there, in that vast space that's big enough for everyone, learn the humility, generosity, and gratitude that makes each one of us essential to the network of life."

Pause

Take a few moments to realize: *You are here, in this moment, in this place.* Rest here. Breathe in Divine love; breathe out your own love, sending it out into the world.

Let yourself experience what it's like to be a "big soul," unfettered by selfishness.

Now look at your life the way it is right now. What things are you already doing that contribute to the well-being of others? It could be something as simple as making dinner for your family—or as big as donating money or volunteering time to a charity. Now consciously think of each of these actions as a connection point with the Spirit of Love. Does this change how you think about doing these things (and if so, how)?

Next, consider if the Spirit might want to lead you into additional activities to demonstrate your creativity, reverence, and stewardship to your fellow humans or the environment. How might the spirit of magnanimity shape your life in new ways?

As you leave this quiet pause in your day, take this question with you. Think about it more deeply over the next few days, and make a note each time thoughts occur to you. Don't listen to guilt or "shoulds," but instead, be open to the generous spiritual energy that is seeking to flow out through your unique skills and resources.

24

Inner Authority

As I practice the principles
of self-awareness and service,
I find true inner authority.

As we form the habit of consciously looking for Divine love in all things, basing our decision-making on the principles Ignatius taught (see chapter 9), we reclaim our own inner authority. We don't give our authority away anymore, allowing the messages we hear on social media, television, and from other aspects of our society to unconsciously shape us, and we no longer feel the need to automatically conform to the expectations of friends and family. We rest in the strength and peace of knowing we are in tune with our own hearts and with the Source of all life. We trust our connection with the Divine and with the world around us.

Inner authority comes from knowing who we truly are. It emerges when we no longer have to constantly prove our own value. It allows us to handle with compassion and care whatever life throws at us. It empowers us to set goals, to take action—and to follow through to the end. It helps us:

- Be patient when dealing with situations that are frustrating or challenging.
- Set healthy boundaries that protect our liberty, even as they are permeable to the demands of love.
- Deal lovingly but firmly with people who threaten to barge through those boundaries (regardless of whether they are employers, colleagues, friends, or family members).
- Persevere as we pursue distant or of difficult goals.
- Overcome the doubts and anxieties that might otherwise hold us back.
- Believe we have the ability to influence the direction of social change.

Our sense of interior authority allows us to recognize and access the opportunities and resources that are available to us. We maintain and cultivate our inner energy, even as we seek to protect and encourage that energy in others.

Inner authority does not mean, however, that we allow our egos to puff up like turkeys. As we work to participate in the Divine Dream, we are sensitive to the presence of our own pride and ambition. We remember that when we participate in activism for justice, the goal is not to make ourselves look good. We consciously and attentively listen to what others have to say, rather than crashing forward like the proverbial bull in the teashop, our actions fueled by our assumptions and pride. As we work to be allies with communities experiencing oppression and unequal access to resources and privileges, we do so with humility, realizing and respecting the richness, strength, and potential these communities already possess. We approach each situation with the child's mind we discussed in chapter 13: the openness to setting aside our own beliefs and the willingness to learn through each encounter.

A story about Jesus in the Gospel of Matthew reveals the contrast between genuine inner authority and the sense of authority that comes from arrogance and selfishness. As the Gospel narrates it, the mother of two of Jesus's close friends, James and John, was ambitious for her two sons; the thought of their importance to Jesus filled her hungry ego with a sense of misguided possibility—and so, dragging her two sons along behind her, she comes to Jesus and kneels before him.

"What do you want?" he asks her.

This woman (and her sons as well) does not yet understand that Jesus is not going to overthrow the Roman occupiers and establish a new political kingdom. And so she says to Jesus, "Make these two sons of mine sit beside you in your government, one on your left side, one on your right side."

Jesus shakes his head and says, "You don't understand what you are asking." He turns to James and John, "Are you able to drink from the cup that I must drink?"

They don't understand he's talking about his own death, his total self-surrender, and so they answer quickly and easily, "We can do that."

Jesus gives them a sad smile. "You will drink from my cup—but I cannot grant you the power you are asking for."

When Jesus's other friends hear about this incident, they're indignant at the two brothers—not because they understand what Jesus is doing any more than James and John do but because they too want power and authority in the government they envision Jesus establishing.

But Jesus gathers his friends around him and explains: "My Dream has nothing to do with the sort of power and authority you are used to thinking about. In the Divine Dream, the greatest person is the person who serves the most. The person with the most authority also has the most humility. You are not here to be served but to serve others— to give your life away out of love. This is the path to true inner authority."

Pause

Rest for a few moments, letting your body and mind become quiet. Be aware of your breath, going in, going out. Allow everything else to drop away from your attention.

When you feel ready, think about the story from the Gospel of Matthew. Here, as he did so often, Jesus turns societal expectations upside down. He tells us that Divine authority is not based on power or prominence but on humility and the commitment to actively give ourselves to the needs of others.

Enter into this scene in your mind, imagining you are one of Jesus's inner circle of close friends. Ever since we were children, we have all wanted to be first, to be at the center, to have the power to tell others what to do. So how do you feel when you hear about James and John asking for prominent positions in what they imagine will be Jesus's political kingdom? Do you talk to your friends about your feelings, gossiping about how awful James and John are? Or do you possess an inner authority that is unconcerned by the clamor of others' egos? Be honest about your emotions and reactions as you put yourself in this situation. Remember, no one is going to judge you!

Now take your feelings to Jesus. Imagine sitting near him and talking with him about what you want most for yourself—your goals and ambitions. Listen for what he says in response. If it's helpful, write this imaginary conversation on paper.

When you have said everything that is in your heart and allowed time to hear what the Spirit of Love might be saying to you through your imagination, return to the rest of your day. Bring this conversation with you, and return to it later in the day when you have a few quiet moments. Look for any new insights. Feel free to continue your conversation with Jesus whenever you have occasion.

25

Moment-by-Moment Presence

I live in the moment-by-moment awareness of the Divine
Presence, opening myself to inner transformation
as I work to bring change and healing
to the world around me.

As his Spiritual Exercises come to a close, Ignatius of Loyola invites us to recall our true identities so that we remain in the stream of Divine love, taking action in whatever ways open to us each day. Our faith in the ongoing work of love is not anchored in the invisible, intangible realms of the "spirit world" but in the presence of the Divine in each aspect of the physical world around us. This awareness becomes a home we take with us wherever we are. Awareness becomes the foundation of our spiritual lives.

According to Jesuit theologian Johann Baptist Metz, Jesus did not teach a spirituality based on the "closed eyes" of traditional prayer but rather a spirituality of "open eyes, which sees more and not less," which "especially makes visible all invisible and inconvenient suffering, and—convenient or not—pays attention to it and takes responsibility for it." Reflected in this spirituality, says Metz, is the Divine Spirit, who is a friend to all human beings.

In Jesus's last words before he said goodbye to his friends, he spoke to them about time. The sense of time he had in mind was not our sequential, linear understanding but rather a concept that is expressed by the Greek word *Kairos*. This is the time of the Divine Dream, the time of opportunity and potential, the moments when linear time intersects with eternity, and amazing possibilities emerge. In the paused moments of meditation and mindfulness, we enter into this time. Although we cannot stay there forever, as we become more aware of the flow of *Kairos* in us and around us, we learn to cooperate with its movements. We "go with the flow" in an active rather than passive way.

Throughout the Spiritual Exercises, Ignatius invites us to think of the spiritual life as something that is never static, that's constantly moving to fulfill the *magis* concept of *better* and *more*. This process goes on both inside us and in the exterior world. As participants in the Divine Dream, Ignatius wrote, we "should have one foot on the ground, and the other raised to proceed on the journey." This stance doesn't permit us to become too attached to any one place or any stage of our spiritual journeys. While we ground ourselves in the wide-awake awareness of the present moment, we are also always ready to surrender that moment and move on.

Each aspect of the Spiritual Exercises propels our movement. The security of unconditional love gives us the confidence we need to step out in new directions. Awareness of our inner thoughts and emotions frees us from being weighed down by them, allowing us to move more lightly.

As we speak with the Something or Someone who lies beyond ourselves, expressing our innermost thoughts and our hearts' desires, we become comfortable connecting our inner lives with both the "spiritual world" and the world of the five senses. In the life of Jesus, we see a model of love, friendship, and community, one that we can imitate in our own lives. We connect our hearts to the Divine through our imagination, even as we use our imagination to see the potential hidden in the world as it is. We learn to make decisions that reflect the Divine messages we receive through our emotions.

At the same time, as we become more aware of others' reality, we hear the call to join in solidarity with all who are marginalized or oppressed. We surrender our arrogance and selfishness, and we respond in humility, with active expressions of compassion. In the cycle of birth-death-new life, we find hope for constructing a way of life built on the foundation of the Divine Dream of healing and possibility for our world. And finally, in each thing we feel and think and do, we seek the presence of love.

In Ignatius's Examen exercise, we experience a form of what's known as "mindfulness meditation"—a state of mind that focuses our awareness on our emotions, thoughts, and physical sensations. We may look both inward at ourselves and outward at the reality of the world, but either way, we let go of our usual preconceptions and judgments. We enter the state of mind where we step outside our egos. The Examen gives us a chance to pause, to be quiet long enough to listen to ourselves, to the Divine, and to the call of justice from the world around us.

Science tells us that this is more than a nice spiritual practice. Daily moments of mindfulness, researchers report, can shrink our inner prejudices by diminishing our negativity bias (our knee-jerk negative reactions to certain situations), by decreasing our anxieties when we encounter people different from ourselves, and by helping us see others not only as our equals but also as people who have unique gifts to offer, gifts we vitally need. The daily practice of mindfulness, research further shows, enhances our compassion, forming new neural connections that lead to active expressions of love.

In the Gospel of Matthew, Jesus says, "The Divine Dream is like a tiny seed. It may be so small you can barely see it—but when it grows, it becomes a tree so tall that birds take shelter in its branches, entire communities of life live in its roots, and it brings beauty to the entire world."

The Divine Dream has infinite potential—but its growth cannot be hurried. Our job is to seek and find its seeds, and then nurture them with care and attention. As Divine love transforms our hearts, we yearn for ever-greater justice. We work and wait for the life-giving transformation of love.

Pause

In the small pauses at the end of each chapter, we have directed our attention at our breath and our bodies. As beginners, it is easier to have something small and precise to focus on. The field of awareness, however, is boundless. You can choose to enter it through any aspect that works for you—your breath, the pattern of sunlight on the floor, the sound of music, the flicker of a candle, the scent of new-cut grass, or the faces of strangers passing by. Reality is so full! It is constantly overflowing, too vast for the messages of our senses and emotions to keep up with it.

As you pause, reach out in awareness as far as your mind can go (without beginning to wander or attach itself to a particular train of thought).

Now allow this boundless field of awareness to enter you. Imagine it is contained within your own heart and mind. In your mind's eye, see it expand until your heart is so spacious it can contain the entire universe. You are not seeking to possess or control anything in the universe; you are simply allowing your awareness to merge with everything that is.

Take a moment to reflect on these thoughts: *Nothing is missing. All is complete. I am complete, and I am one with the universe. Love weaves everything together.*

If your mind resists staying in this place that has no boundaries, you can once again focus on a single aspect of the reality around you . . . and then shift back to the expanded vision that makes room for absolutely everything.

Rest in the quiet *Kairos* moment as long as you can. Leave it with the resolution to return there often. Make greater love your constant goal.

Appendix

Praying the Examen with Our Hands

1 ▲ Acknowledge Divine unconditional love ⚓ Pause to express my needs ▼ Release my intentions

2 ▲ Bring openness to Divine presence ⚓ Pause and affirm Divine presence ▼ Release my observations

3 ▲ Recognize moments of love, encouragement ⚓ Pause with gratitude for this love, encouragement ▼ Release my recognitions, with thanks

4 ▲ Shift awareness to emotions that may arise ⚓ Pause, scanning my body for tension, pain or fear ▼ Release painful emotions

5 ▲ Bring hope for the future ⚓ Pause, asking for Divine direction ▼ Ready myself for loving action

There are different ways to pray the Examen. Below is a tool I invented that helps me focus, physically, emotionally, and spiritually, as I pray the Ignatian Examen. You have probably heard of "muscle memory," the concept that our bodies remember how to do certain behaviors without our minds' conscious direction, but educational research has extended this idea to mean, in effect, that our muscles are virtually extensions of our brains.

When we move our bodies—even in such a simple way as I'm about to describe—we expand our mental capacity as well. This "embodied cognition" turns symbolic or purely intellectual concepts into physical realities. Like focusing on your breathing, focusing on your fingers is a way to embody prayer. Practices like these help us balance our nervous systems, creating a greater sense of calm and freedom from stress, but they are also another way to connect us with the Divine.

In this practice, we use our five fingers as physical anchors for the Examen's five steps. Before we begin, we bring an "intention" to the Examen. This might be a need you are feeling, either for yourself, for a loved one, or for the larger community in which you participate, or it might be a decision you are struggling to make. Whatever it is, hold it as your focus as you breathe in . . . and out. Do this five times, once for each finger on your hand.

1. Begin the Examen by placing your right index finger at the base of your left thumb. Inhale as you slowly slide your finger from the base of your thumb to the tip of your thumb while expressing your confidence that in your need, you are unconditionally loved by the Divine. At the tip of your thumb, hold your breath for five seconds as you express your "intention" for this pause in your day. Put into words the need you are bringing to this time. Then, as you let your finger slide down the opposite side of your thumb, release your breath.

2. As you slide your right index finger up your left index finger, open your awareness to the Divine Presence. You may perceive this emotionally—or perhaps not. Either way, the Divine is with you. As your right finger reaches the tip of your left finger, pause for five seconds, holding your breath while you affirm that Divinity is present in all things, including the specific things you see, feel, smell, taste, and hear in this moment. Then, as you exhale, slowly slide your right index finger down

your left index finger until it rests between that finger and your left middle finger.

3. As you inhale, sliding your right index finger up from the base of your left middle finger to the tip, look back and recognize all the ways you have felt loved, encouraged, and strengthened over the past week (or day, or month—you can choose the time period, but make it short enough that you can bring to mind specific events). At the tip of your middle finger, hold your breath for five seconds, expressing your gratitude for all the demonstrations of love in your life. Then release your breath as your right finger slides down between your left middle finger and your left ring finger.

4. Inhale while sliding your right index finger up your left ring finger, at the same time shifting your awareness to your emotions, whatever they are in this moment. At the tip of the finger, pause and hold your breath for five seconds while scanning your body for any pain or tension connected to your emotions. As you exhale, sliding your finger down between your ring finger and little finger, affirm to yourself that all tension, sorrow, or fear is flowing out from you.

5. Finally, as you slide your right index finger up your left little finger, inhale while affirming that you are breathing

in hope for the future. Pause, holding your breath for five seconds at the tip of your little finger. During this pause, ask for Divine direction. As you exhale, your finger sliding down your little finger, express your openness for actively expressing love in your actions during the rest of the day (or the coming days).

Notes

Scripture quotations, unless noted as paraphrased, are from The Voice™. Copyright © 2008 by Ecclesia Bible Society. Used by permission. All rights reserved.

Quotations from *The Spiritual Exercises* are from *The Spiritual Exercises of St. Ignatius of Loyola* (Charlotte, NC: TAN Books, 1999). In some cases, I have paraphrased the wording to make it more compatible with modern and inclusive language.

Introduction

The quote by Ann Weiser Cornel is from *The Radical Acceptance of Everything: Living a Focusing Life* (Wareham, UK: Calluna, 2005), 11.

In *The Red Book* (New York: Doubleday, 2009), Jung writes, "Through uniting with the self we reach God" (p. 338).

William Watson is the author of *Sacred Story: An Ignatian Examen for the Third Millenium* (Seattle, WA: Sacred Story Press, 2012).

Pedro Arrupe was the Superior General of the Jesuits from 1965 to 1983. According to IgnatianSpirituality.com, the actual source of the quote that's always attributed to him is Joseph Whelan, an American Jesuit who was assistant to the Superior General of the Jesuits in Rome in the 1980s.

Chapter 3

For more information about Islam and self-awareness, see: https://khalilcenter.com/articles/four-benefits-of-cultivating-self-awareness.

For more about Hinduism and self-awareness, see: https://www.hinduismtoday.com/hindu-basics/god-soul-and-world/.

The Scripture reference to examining ourselves is in 2 Corinthians 13:5, and 2 Corinthians 5:10 speaks of taking every thought captive.

To find out more about Paganism and embodied knowing, read "The Knowing Body" by Adrian Paul Harris in *Contributions to Law, Philosophy and Ecology: Exploring Re-Embodiments,* Ruth Thomas-Pellicer, Vito De Lucia, and Sian Sullivan, eds. (New York: Routledge, 2016), 139–58.

Tricycle's "Buddhism for Beginners" (https://tricycle.org/beginners/buddhism/what-is-mindfulness/) explains the Buddha's understanding of mindfulness.

The quotation from Allan Fenigstein is from his article "Public and
Private Self-Consciousness: Assessment and Theory," *Journal of Consulting and Clinical Psychology* 43, no. 4 (1975):
522–27, https://doi.org/10.1037/h0076760.

The Gospel of Thomas is a collection of 114 pithy sayings attributed to Jesus. Scholars believe it may have been written
earlier than the other four Gospels, and many Bible scholars
see it as a valuable resource for understanding the historical Jesus. It is not, however, a part of the church-authorized
"canon" of the Bible, and the Catholic Church, as well as
many conservative Protestant groups, do not recognize it as
a genuine Gospel.

Chapter 4

Many psychologists have added "freeze" to the fight-or-flight
response since that is a common response to hyperarousal in
the modern world.

Chapter 5

The quote from Barry and Ann Ulanov is from their book *Primary
Speech: A Psychology of Prayer* (Louisville, KY: Westminster
John Knox, 1982), 9.

Chapter 6

The reference to Jesus being born "outside the city gate" is from Hebrews 13:12.

Chapter 7

To learn more about the science behind the uses of the imagination mentioned in this chapter, see: Steven Roy Mann, "Sports and the Imagination," *Sports and the Mind*, September 25, 2022, https://sportsandthemind.com/; University of Colorado, "Your Brain on Imagination: It's a Lot Like Reality, Study Shows," *Science Daily*, December 10, 2018, https://www.sciencedaily.com/; D. L. Schacter, D. R. Addis, D. Hassabis, et al., "The Future of Memory: Remembering, Imagining, and the Brain," *Neuron* 76, no. 4 (November 21, 2012): 677–94, https://www.ncbi.nlm.nih.gov/pmc/articles/PMC3815616/.

Chapter 10

See Julian Hoffman's book *The Small Heart of Things: Being at Home in a Beckoning World* (Athens: University of Georgia Press, 2013) for more on the interconnection of the natural and human worlds.

Chapter 11

The story that Jesus tells about the host is from Matthew 25:35–
40. This is a paraphrase of the Scripture passage.

The reference to Kelly Brown Douglas is a paraphrase of an interview she did for *Sojourner's Magazine*, July 2020.

Father Greg Boyle's quote is from his book *Barking to the Choir:
The Power of Radical Kinship* (New York: Simon & Schuster,
2017), 12.

Chapter 12

The story Jesus tells about the neighbor (the story often referred
to as "The Good Samaritan") is paraphrased from Luke
10:25–37.

The material from Beverly Tatum is from "Lighting Candles in
the Dark: One Black Woman's Response to White Antira-
cist Narratives" in *Becoming and Unbecoming White: Owning
and Disowning a Racial Identity*, Christine Clark and James
O'Donnell, eds. (Westport, CT: Bergin & Garvey, 1999).
Tatum has expanded these ideas about racial identity in her
more recent book *Why Are All the Black Kids Sitting Together
in the Cafeteria?: And Other Conversations About Race* (New
York: Basic, 2017).

Janet Helm's research material is from *Black and White Racial Identity: Theory, Research and Practice* (Westport, CT: Greenwood Press, 1990).

The quote from Elie Wiesel is from an interview in *U.S. News and World Report*, October 27, 1986.

The quotations from Oscar Romero are found in *Theological Vision: Liberation and the Transfiguration of the Poor* by Edgardo Colón-Emeric (Notre Dame, IN: University of Notre Dame Press, 2018).

Dorothy Day's quote is found in *Love Is the Measure: A Biography of Dorothy Day* (Maryknoll, NY: Orbis, 1986), 33.

Gustavo Gutiérrez's quote is from *The Power of the Poor in History* (Eugene, OR: Wipf & Stock, 2004), 45.

Chapter 13

You can read more about Frances de Sales's spirituality in his *Introduction to the Devout Life* (Savage, MN: BroadStreet, 2007). The quote in this chapter is from page 60.

Research on humility can be found here: https://www.psychologytoday.com/us/blog/the-art-self-improvement/202006/the-art-humility.

Chapter 14

You can find a collection of research articles on empathy and compassion at Stanford Medicine's Center for Compassion and Altruism Research and Education, http://ccare.stanford. edu/research/current-research/.

The Charter for Compassion is from http://charterforcompassion. org. I added the parenthetical material to help apply the charter to this book's focus. If you go to the website, you'll have an opportunity to add your name to the charter. You'll also find a printable PDF version of the charter for you to share.

The quote from Glennon Doyle is from her blog post on July 7, 2014, Glennon Doyle Melton, "How to Really Change Your Children's Lives This Summer," HuffPost, https://www. huffpost.com/entry/how-to-really-change-your-childrens-lives-this-summer_b_5538863.

Chapter 15

Jesus's discussion of the seed is found in John 12:24.

Chapter 18

Swordplay and violence were common in Ignatius's day, and in his youth, he often participated in fights. One night, for example, he and his brothers ambushed and assaulted a group of men, and as a result, Ignatius had to flee town. He was finally brought to justice, but the case against him was dropped, thanks to his powerful family's influence.

Chapter 19

Jesus's "dream" is paraphrased from John 17:21–23.

Paul's description of the spiritual body is found in 1 Corinthians 12:12–17, 19–22, 24–27.

Howard Thurman's quote is from *Disciplines of the Spirit* (Richmond, IN: Friends United, 1977), 27.

Chapter 20

Gustavo Gutiérrez's quote is from his *Essential Writings* (Minneapolis: Fortress, 1996), 229.

Jürgen Moltmann. *Theology of Hope: On the Ground and the Implications of a Christian Eschatology* (New York: Harper & Row, 1967), 20.

Chapter 21

Romans 8:28 is the reference for the apostle Paul's promise that all things will work together for good as we participate in Divine love.

Jack Kornfield is an American author, teacher, and practitioner of Buddhism. He has written many books on meditation, including *The Art of Forgiveness, Lovingkindness, and Peace* (New York: Bantam, 2008), *Bringing Home the Dharma: Awakening Right Where You Are* (Boulder, CO: Shambhala, 2011), and *A Lamp in the Darkness: Illuminating the Path Through Difficult Times* (Boulder, CO: Sounds True, 2014).

Chapter 24

The story about the two brothers and their mother coming to Jesus is found in Mark 10:35–45. I have paraphrased that account.

Chapter 25

The quote by Johann Baptist Metz is from his *A Passion for God: The Mystical-Political Dimension of Christianity*, J. Matthew Ashley, trans. (Mahwah, NJ: Paulist Press, 1998), 163.

To find out more about mindfulness research, see "The Science of Mindfulness," Mindful, August 31, 2022, https://www.mindful.org/the-science-of-mindfulness/.